W9-BEB-439

Our Sunday Visitor's

Catholic Encyclopedia for Children

Ann Ball with **Julianne M. Will**

Illustrated by **Kevin Davidson**

Our Sunday Visitor Publishing Division
Our Sunday Visitor, Inc.
Huntington, Indiana 46750

Nihil Obstat: Rev. Michael Heintz
Censor Librorum
Imprimatur: ✠ John D'Arcy
Bishop of Fort Wayne-South Bend
June 26, 2003

The *Nihil Obstat* and *Imprimatur* are declarations that a work is considered free from doctrinal or moral error. It is not implied that those who have granted the same agree with the contents, opinions, or statements expressed.

The Scripture citations used in this work are taken from the *Catholic Edition of the Revised Standard Version of the Bible* (RSV), copyright © 1965 and 1966 by the Division of Christian Education of the National Council of the Churches of Christ in the United States of America. Used by permission. All rights reserved.

Every reasonable effort has been made to determine copyright holders of excerpted materials and to secure permissions as needed. If any copyrighted materials have been inadvertently used in this work without proper credit being given in one form or another, please notify Our Sunday Visitor in writing so that future printings of this work may be corrected accordingly.

Copyright © 2003 by Our Sunday Visitor Publishing Division, Our Sunday Visitor, Inc.

All rights reserved. With the exception of short excerpts for critical reviews, no part of this work may be reproduced or transmitted in any form or by any means whatsoever without permission in writing from the publisher. Write:

Our Sunday Visitor Publishing Division
Our Sunday Visitor, Inc.
200 Noll Plaza
Huntington, IN 46750

ISBN: 1-931709-86-6 (Inventory No. R41)

Cover design by Kevin Davidson
Interior design by Rebecca Heaston

PRINTED IN THE UNITED STATES OF AMERICA

Contents

FOREWORD

When I am preaching a homily to children, I always find that the adults in the congregation seem to be enjoying the homily as much as the young ones. In reading this *Catholic Encyclopedia for Children*, I felt like an adult eavesdropping on children discovering the wonderful world of God. Kevin Davidson's artwork portrays the colorful stories of the Bible, the dramatic tales of Church history, the engaging lives of saints, and the vivid rituals of the sacraments in an appealing, captivating way.

Ann Ball and Julianne Will excel in the craft of storytelling in this most readable text. They know that for children, one needs to cut to the chase and allow the marvelous stories of faith work their own magic on the imaginations of the young. The union of picture and text is satisfying in the same way that the lyrics and melodies of a good song touch the heart.

I think that parents, grandparents, and teachers will enjoy reading this book to children. Children's eyes will fill with wonder when they hear and see this great story of faith. They will want to read themselves. This book will be a valued supplement to the study of religion in Catholic schools and parish education programs. I liked it. I believe you will as well.

— Rev. Alfred McBride, O.Praem.

THERE ARE SO MANY FUN THINGS FOR ME TO TELL YOU ABOUT!

Hello, kids!

Welcome! This book was written just for you. It will answer some of your questions and help you learn more about our wonderful Catholic faith.

Meet Ichthus (Ik' thus). He is a Christian fish. You'll see Ichthus swimming around as you read through this book. At the end, you'll find out how he got his name and what it means. We hope you enjoy these stories and drawings, and discover just how great God's love is. So follow Ichthus as we dive right in!

Your friends,

Ann, Julianne, and Kevin

The Writers and The Artist

A special thank you to Austin Wilken, who served as junior editor on this project.

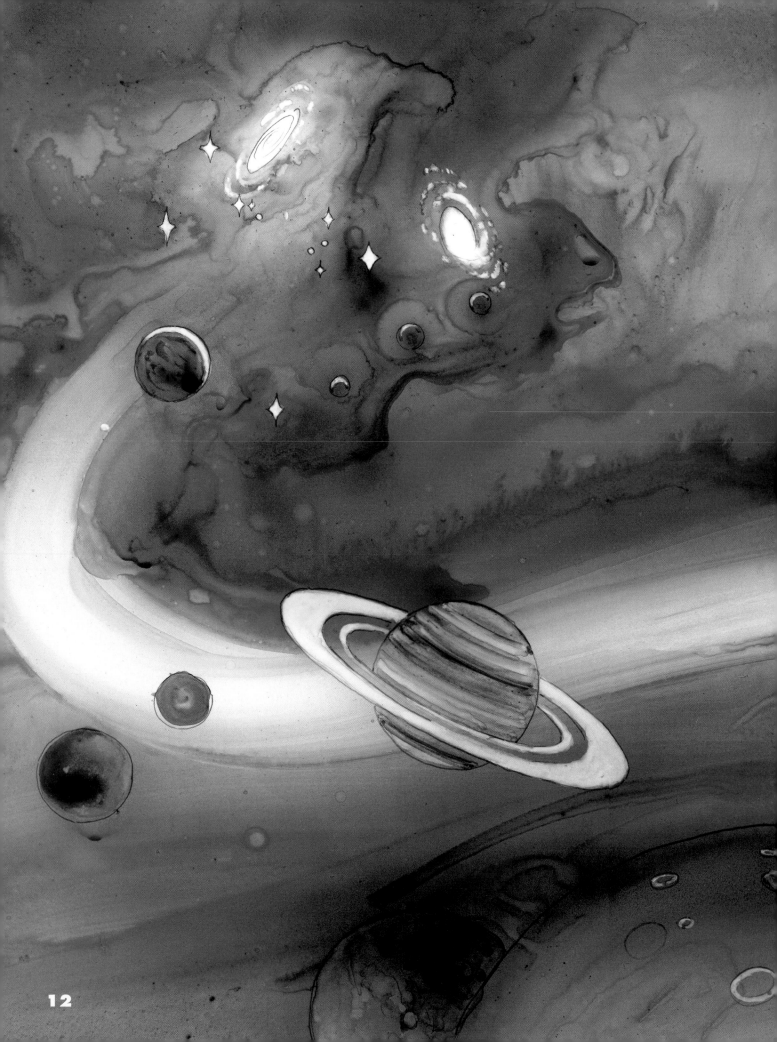

I.

IN THE BEGINNING

THE BIBLE: THE STORY OF GOD'S LOVE FOR US

God made us and loves us. He wants us to follow him and to live with him forever. God wants us to get to know him.

How do we know about God's love and his promises to us? A very special book called the Bible tells us about God and his plan. The Bible is a story of God's love for us. This holy book was written long ago, in the time before and after Jesus was here on earth.

The Bible is also called "Scripture," and it is really many books combined into one. Many different writers wrote these books, but each wrote with God's help. We call that help "inspiration."

These books of the Bible are split up into two parts, or testaments. The word "testament" means "truth-telling." The books of the Old Testament describe how God created the world and all that happened in the world until Jesus was born. The books of the New Testament tell about Jesus' time on earth and his lessons on how to live in heaven with him.

THE REST OF THE STORY

The Bible is a great and holy book. But it's not the only way to learn about God's wonderful love for us. Jesus told his friends, called "apostles," to go tell everyone about God's love. Some of the apostles wrote down this message in the Bible. But some of the apostles traveled and talked about God's plan. Their teachings are called Sacred, or Apostolic, Tradition.

We believe this Tradition is the truth about God and his plan. The Tradition that Jesus taught the apostles does not change. Our Sacred Tradition and our Sacred Scripture teach us all that we need to know about God's love for us. They tell us how we should love God so that we can live with him forever.

WE ARE SURROUNDED BY GIFTS FROM GOD.

GOD CREATED THE WORLD
(Genesis 1:1-31)

In the beginning, there was only God. Everything was dark before God created heaven and earth.

Then God said "Let there be light," and there was light. He called the light "day," and he called the darkness "night." This was the first day.

Second, God made the beautiful sky, and he separated it from the world below.

Third, God created water and land. He made many plants and trees, too, and they grew wonderful fruit.

Next, God made the sun, the moon, and the stars, and put them in the sky. God looked at what he had done and saw how great it was.

Then God made all kinds of fish and birds and animals to live on the land and in the water. He made them able to have baby fish and birds and animals, so they could fill the wonderful world he had made.

God looked at what he had made and saw how beautiful it was. He wanted to share his beautiful creation and his love with someone like himself. So God made the first man and woman to live on his earth and to share his love. He called the first man Adam and the first woman Eve. God told them to marry and have children, and to enjoy the things he had made.

At last, God was finished. He looked at what he had done, and it was very good. So on the seventh day, he rested.

God blessed the seventh day, now called Sunday. He made it a holy day to rest from work, a day to relax and enjoy all the good things God has given us.

EDEN: THE BEAUTIFUL GARDEN
(Genesis 2:4-25; 3)

God made a beautiful garden in Eden and gave it to Adam and Eve, our first parents. In the center of the garden was a tree with very special fruit. The person who ate that fruit would know what was good and evil.

God allowed Adam and Eve to eat the fruit of any tree in the garden, except that tree with the special fruit. God told them they could not even touch the tree of knowledge, or they would die.

But there was a serpent in the garden. He tempted Eve, telling her that the fruit from the tree of knowledge was the sweetest fruit in the garden. The serpent said if she ate it, she would be like a god, because she would know good and evil.

Eve ate the fruit and gave some of it to Adam. Adam and Eve knew that they had disobeyed God and tried to hide. But God knows everything, and Adam and Eve could not hide from him.

When God saw that Adam and Eve had disobeyed him, he sent them out of the beautiful garden. He told them that they would have to work hard for food now. God punished the serpent, too, making it crawl on its belly.

Adam and Eve left the beautiful garden to go work in the world. They had children, and their children had children, and their children's children had children. Soon many people lived on the earth. Adam and Eve were banned from the garden of Eden.

Sin and God's Mercy

Sin is disobedience to God's will. When we do something wrong, our sin offends God. But God loves us very much and is willing to forgive us when we are sorry. If we confess our sins, apologize to those we hurt and to God, and try to do better, God will show us his mercy. His Son, Jesus, died on the cross for our sins, and God wants us to be with him in heaven.

NOAH AND THE GIANT FLOOD
(Genesis 6-8)

The children and grandchildren of Adam and Eve had filled the earth. But many of them were very wicked, mean people, destroying God's beautiful work, and God grew very sad. Only one man, Noah, was good and obeyed God.

God told Noah that he had decided to flood the earth to wash away everything evil. He asked Noah to build a huge boat, called an "ark," that Noah and his family could live on until the floodwaters went down. God told Noah to bring birds and animals, too. "You shall bring two of every sort into the ark, to keep them alive with you," God said. "Also take with you every sort of food that is eaten, and store it up; and it shall serve as food for you and for them."

Noah made a huge ark for his family and filled it with animals and food. Soon, the rain began to fall. It rained, and rained, and rained – for forty days and forty nights, it rained. Finally the rain stopped, but Noah and his family floated on the sea in the ark full of animals for many days afterward.

At last God created a strong wind to begin drying the earth. Noah sent a dove out of the ark to see whether it could find dry land. The dove came back with a branch from an olive tree in its mouth. Now Noah, his family, and the animals could leave the ark.

Noah's children had children and grandchildren. Soon the earth was full of Noah's descendants, as well as many birds and animals. God made a promise to Noah, a "covenant": He would never flood the earth again.

God Tests Abraham
(Genesis 12-22)

Abraham, a descendant of Noah, lived with his wife, Sarah, in Haran. Abraham and Sarah wanted children very much, but were sad because God had not sent them any.

One day, God told Abraham to leave Haran. He promised Abraham many blessings if he obeyed, and said he would have as many descendants as there were stars in the sky. Abraham did not understand how Sarah, who was very old, could have a baby, but he trusted God and obeyed him. Abraham and Sarah left Haran and traveled to a place called Canaan. Abraham built an altar there for God. God blessed him, and Abraham became very rich.

Then, just as God had promised, Sarah had a baby. Abraham and Sarah were overjoyed. They loved their son, Isaac, very much.

When Isaac grew older, God decided to test Abraham to see just how much he loved God, and whether he would still obey. God told Abraham to take Isaac out to the desert and kill him as a sacrifice to God.

Abraham was terribly sad. How could he hurt his son, whom he loved so very much? But Abraham loved God more and trusted him, so he took Isaac out to the desert. Abraham prepared to kill Isaac as God had asked.

Suddenly, God sent an angel to stop Abraham. He had passed the test! God saw that Abraham loved him enough even to give up his only son. Abraham loved Isaac very much, but he loved God first.

Abraham was filled with joy – he could keep his son! God promised Abraham and his family many blessings. Abraham and Isaac left the desert together and went home to Sarah.

God kept his promise, called a "covenant," because Abraham obeyed God. He sent many blessings to Abraham and Isaac, and Isaac's children, and their children, and all the descendents of Abraham.

23

JOSEPH'S COAT OF MANY COLORS
(Genesis 37-45)

Isaac's son Jacob had twelve boys. All worked together as shepherds, tending their family sheep. Jacob loved all his sons. But Joseph was Jacob's favorite. Jacob gave Joseph a beautiful coat of many colors. The other sons grew very jealous of Joseph and his beautiful new coat.

They also were angry with Joseph because of the dreams he had been having. In one dream Joseph saw the sun, the moon, and eleven stars bowing down to him. His brothers said it sounded like Joseph expected them to bow down to him. They grew even angrier.

One day the brothers were working in the field when Joseph came with a message from their father. The brothers saw Joseph coming in his beautiful coat and became so angry and jealous that they thought about killing him. Instead, they sold Joseph to some travelers who wanted to put Joseph to work in Egypt. They tore the beautiful coat his father had given him. Joseph's father thought Joseph was dead, and he was very sad.

Joseph was a good worker, and almost everyone who knew him in Egypt liked him. But one day he met a mean woman who grew angry when he would not do the bad things she wanted him to do. So she made up a terrible lie about him and had Joseph put in jail.

While Joseph was in jail, his friends there talked to him about their dreams. Joseph had a gift for dreams. He was able to tell his friends what their dreams meant, and what would happen in the future. Everyone was excited about Joseph's gift, and soon he was famous.

One night the ruler of the land, called the "pharaoh," had a dream that no one could understand. So the pharaoh called Joseph out of jail and asked him what his dream meant.

Joseph explained that soon there would be a famine. There would not be enough food for everyone unless they were very careful and saved extra food for the next few years.

The pharaoh was impressed with this wise young man. He put Joseph in charge of storing the food for Egypt. Joseph became one of the pharaoh's good friends.

Seven years later there was a great famine, just as Joseph had said. Egypt was the only land that had food, thanks to Joseph, who had stored more than enough.

But in Canaan, Joseph's father and brothers quickly ran out things to eat. Jacob sent his sons to Egypt to buy grain. They didn't know it was their brother Joseph in charge of the grain, but he recognized his brothers at once. He put them in jail.

The brothers talked among themselves there in jail. They said this was a punishment from God for the mean thing they had done to their brother Joseph many years ago. They said they were sorry for their sin. When Joseph heard this, he was very happy.

After Joseph was sure his brothers were truly sorry, he surprised them by telling them, "I am your brother, Joseph, whom you sold into Egypt. And now do not be distressed, or angry with yourselves, because you sold me here; for God sent me before you to preserve life." This shocked the brothers, because now Joseph was a very powerful friend of the pharaoh.

The brothers were very, very happy to see Joseph. They hurried home to tell their father, Jacob, that Joseph was alive. He was overjoyed, and the whole family moved to Egypt.

MOSES AND THE GREAT ESCAPE
(Exodus 1-14)

After the death of the kind pharaoh who became Joseph's friend, an evil man took his place as leader of Egypt. This pharaoh was very jealous of Joseph's descendants, the Israelites. He made them slaves of the Egyptians, and told his soldiers to kill all their baby boys.

One mother hid her baby boy from the soldiers. She put him in a basket at the edge of the river, where he would be safe. Soon, the pharaoh's daughter came to the river and found the baby boy. She decided to take him home and name him Moses, which means "pulled out of the water."

Moses grew up in the pharaoh's palace, strong and healthy and good. Because he had a loving heart, Moses grew angry when he saw one of the pharaoh's soldiers hurting an Israelite slave. He told the soldier to stop hurting the man, but the soldier didn't listen. To save the slave, Moses killed the soldier. Moses knew the pharaoh would punish him for this, so he ran away to a different land and became a shepherd.

Moses was out in the field caring for his sheep when he suddenly saw a burning bush. He went to investigate and was surprised to see that the leaves stayed green! Then he realized that God was speaking to him.

God told Moses that the Israelites were suffering in Egypt as the slaves of the pharaoh. "I will send you to Pharaoh that you may bring forth my people, the sons of Israel, out of Egypt," God said.

Moses was afraid. "Who am I that I should go to Pharaoh and bring the sons of Israel out of Egypt?" he said.

But God told Moses that he would help him perform many miracles to make the pharaoh listen. So Moses and his brother Aaron went to Egypt to free the Israelites.

When Moses went before the pharaoh and told him to let God's people go, Pharaoh said, "I do not know the LORD, and moreover I will not let Israel go."

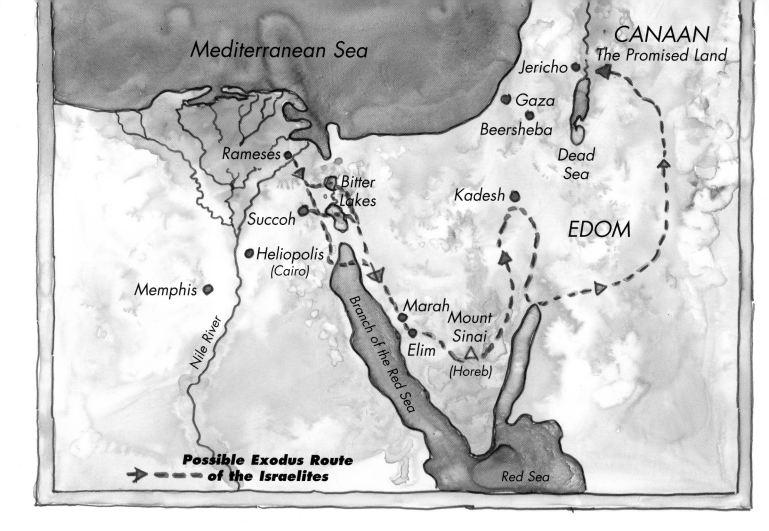

Map labels: Mediterranean Sea, CANAAN The Promised Land, Jericho, Gaza, Beersheba, Dead Sea, Rameses, Bitter Lakes, Kadesh, EDOM, Succoh, Heliopolis (Cairo), Memphis, Nile River, Branch of the Red Sea, Marah, Mount Sinai, Elim, (Horeb), Red Sea

Possible Exodus Route of the Israelites

Moses threw his walking stick on the ground, and it turned into a snake. The pharaoh was surprised, but he refused to set the slaves free.

The next day, Moses and Aaron met the pharaoh by the river and asked him again to let the people go. Again, Pharaoh refused. This time, Aaron threw his stick in the river, and the water turned to blood! This made the pharaoh angry because no one could drink the water, so he began to punish the Israelites even more.

Nine more times, Moses told the pharaoh to let his people go. Nine more times, Pharaoh refused. Nine times, bad things happened to the Egyptians. Frogs and locusts covered the land. The sky became dark, and the sun did not shine. Each time, the pharaoh would become frightened and promise to let the Israelites go. But each time, as soon as the problem was over, he changed his mind.

Finally, God told Moses that the Israelites should mark their doors with a special sign. That night, the Angel of Death came to Egypt. It took the oldest child of each Egyptian family, but passed by the Israelites' houses marked with the sign.

The Angel of Death even took the pharaoh's son. This was too much for the pharaoh, and he told Moses to take the Israelites out of Egypt. Quickly the Israelites headed off toward the Red Sea before Pharaoh could change his mind again.

Soon the pharaoh became angry. He wanted to punish the Israelites, and he sent his large army to bring them back.

How frightened the Israelites were! The sea was in front of them, and the army was behind them. Moses asked God what to do. Suddenly, a dark cloud came down and the Egyptian army could not see the Israelites!

God told Moses to hold his hand out over the Red Sea. A strong wind came and blew the water aside, making a dry path so the Israelites could cross over. Quickly, they ran across to safety. Then God told Moses to hold his hand over the sea again. Just as the Egyptian army got to the middle of the path across the sea, the waters rushed back, washing away the army.

The Israelites were saved. At last God's people were free!

The night when the Angel of Death passed by the Israelites' homes is called "Passover." Even today Hebrew people all over the world celebrate the night their children were saved.

A STRONG WIND BLEW THE WATER ASIDE.

THE TEN COMMANDMENTS
(Exodus 16-20)

After Moses led the Israelites across the Red Sea, they found themselves in a large wilderness. The people began to worry, because there was no food. But the Lord spoke to Moses, and Moses reminded the people to trust God. He told them that God had promised to lead them to a new land, full of milk and honey and all good things.

The people said their prayers, and feeling sad, tired, and hungry, they went to bed. What would happen to them?

What a surprise! The next morning there were strange white flakes all over the ground. The people asked Moses what the white flakes were. "It is the bread which the LORD has given you to eat," replied Moses. The people gathered the strange new food, called "manna," and ate it. God would not let them starve!

While the Israelites were in the wilderness, God called Moses to the top of a mountain and gave him ten rules. These rules are the Ten Commandments, sometimes called the Decalogue. They tell God's people how to behave. We still follow these rules today.

God told Moses that those who obeyed his commandments would be blessed.

Many years later, the Israelites reached the land God promised, full of milk and honey and all good things. Their trust in God was rewarded.

THE TEN COMMANDMENTS TELL GOD'S PEOPLE HOW TO LIVE.

The Ten Commandments

First, I must honor God.

Second, honor his name.

Third, honor his day, keep holy, that will be my aim.

Fourth, I must be obedient.

Fifth, be kind and true.

Sixth, be pure in all I say and see and hear and do.

Seventh, I must be honest.

Eighth, be truthful in all things I say.

Ninth, be pure in mind and heart and all the things I desire each day.

Tenth, I must be satisfied, not be jealous come what may.

These are God's Ten Commandments ...

these I must obey.

— Author unknown

DAVID, THE KING WHO SANG
(1 Samuel 16:14 –1 Samuel 31; 2 Samuel 1-5)

King Saul was very sad. He had not been a good king for the Israelites, and he had disobeyed God. Saul asked his servants to find someone to cheer him up.

Saul's servant brought David, a young shepherd boy who often sang to his sheep to keep them quiet. David sang and played music for Saul, which made him very happy.

At this time the Israelites were fighting another group called the Philistines. The Philistines had a very strong, very large soldier named Goliath, who told the Israelites to send a man to fight him. But the Israelites were afraid of the giant.

David was delivering food to his brothers on the battlefield when he heard Goliath roar out his challenge. David did not like to see the Israelites so frightened by the giant, so he said he would fight him.

"No," said King Saul. "You are but a youth, and he has been a man of war."

But David was not afraid. "The LORD who delivered me from the paw of the lion and from the paw of the bear, will deliver me from the hand of this Philistine."

Sadly, King Saul agreed to let the brave young boy fight. He gave him a sword and the clothes of a soldier. But David did not like the soldier's clothes and the sword. Instead he chose a slingshot and five smooth stones.

As the giant raced toward David with his mighty sword, David used his slingshot to shoot a stone at Goliath. The rock hit the giant smack in the middle of the forehead and knocked him down at once.

When the Philistines saw what happened, they ran and left the Israelites in peace. Young David was a hero.

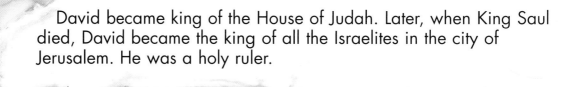

David became king of the House of Judah. Later, when King Saul died, David became the king of all the Israelites in the city of Jerusalem. He was a holy ruler.

David never forgot the days when he was a shepherd boy and sang many beautiful songs honoring God. The words to some of David's songs are written in the Bible, where we can read them today. David's songs are called the Psalms.

One of David's songs compares God to a good shepherd who takes care of his sheep.

The LORD is my shepherd, I shall not want;
He makes me lie down in green pastures.
He leads me beside still waters;
He restores my soul.
He leads me in paths of righteousness for his name's sake.
Even though I walk through the valley of the shadow of death, I fear no evil;
For thou art with me;
Thy rod and thy staff, they comfort me.
Thou preparest a table before me in the presence of my enemies;
thou anointest my head with oil, my cup overflows.
Surely goodness and mercy shall follow me all the days of my life;
And I shall dwell in the house of the LORD for ever.

IN THE BIBLE, DAVID'S SONGS ARE CALLED THE PSALMS.

II.

THE LIFE OF JESUS

GOD KEEPS HIS PROMISES.

THE ANNUNCIATION: AN ANGEL BRINGS GOOD NEWS
(Luke 1:26-38; Matthew 1:18-25)

After Adam and Eve disobeyed God in the garden of Eden, every person was born in the shadow of their sin.

God's people waited and prayed for the day when he would send his Son to make up for this sin, so we could be in heaven with God. They believed that God's Son would come into the world as a mighty king. But God had other plans. He wanted to teach his people about his love.

In the little town of Nazareth, there lived a beautiful girl named Mary. She was from a poor and simple family that loved God very much. Mary did not know it, but God had chosen her to be the mother of his Son. From the minute Mary began to grow in her mother's womb, her soul was clean and pure. She was the only person without the shadow of sin. This was the Immaculate Conception.

Mary became engaged to marry a man named Joseph. Joseph was a carpenter, a person who builds things from wood. He was a poor, simple, good man, who was happy to be marrying such a beautiful and holy girl.

One day before the wedding, an angel named Gabriel appeared to Mary. The angel greeted her and told her some wonderful news. God had chosen her to be the mother of his Son! Today, we remember the angel's words when we say the prayer known as the Hail Mary.

The Hail Mary

Hail Mary, full of grace!
The Lord is with you.
Blessed are you among women,
and blessed is the fruit of your womb,
Jesus.
Holy Mary,
Mother of God,
pray for us sinners,
now and at the hour of our death.
Amen.

Mary was very surprised by the angel's news. But she loved God very much, so she said yes. She agreed to do whatever God asked. We call this her "fiat," which means "Let it be done."

When Joseph found out that Mary was going to have a baby, he was sad. He thought Mary loved another man instead of him. That night, he went to sleep feeling very bad.

But in the middle of the night, an angel came to Joseph. The angel told Joseph that he should go ahead with the wedding. He said that the baby was the Son of God. The angel even told Joseph to name the boy Jesus. He told Joseph to love Mary and the baby and to take care of them all his life. And that is just what Joseph did. We honor Joseph as a saint because he was a good father on earth to our Lord.

When Joseph woke up, he was full of joy. He took Mary as his wife, and they began to make their little home in Nazareth ready for the birth of Jesus.

THE VISITATION: MARY AND ELIZABETH
(Luke 1)

Zechariah was a holy priest who served in the temple. He and his wife, Elizabeth, were good people who loved God very much. But they were sad because they did not have any children. They were old now, and thought it was too late to have a baby.

One day while Zechariah was in the temple, the angel Gabriel came to him and told him that Elizabeth would have a son.

"How shall I know this?" Zechariah said. "For I am an old man, and my wife is advanced in years."

"I am Gabriel, who stand in the presence of God," the angel answered. "You will be silent and unable to speak until the day that these things come to pass, because you did not believe my words, which will be fulfilled in their time."

Zechariah was very surprised at the angel's words. He was even more surprised when he left the temple and could not speak, just as the angel said.

Elizabeth soon learned that she was going to have a baby. She was very happy and thanked God for blessing her. She was to have a son, named John, just as the angel said.

Elizabeth and Mary were cousins. When Mary heard about Elizabeth's baby, she was full of joy for her cousin. Mary decided to visit, to share Elizabeth's happiness and see whether she needed help.

Mary walked to Zechariah and Elizabeth's home in the country. When she saw Elizabeth standing near her house, Mary ran to hug her. Just as Mary came near, the baby in Elizabeth's womb jumped. Elizabeth knew then that Mary was going to have a baby, too. Elizabeth knew that her own son, John, would honor Mary's baby, the Son of God. Elizabeth was filled with the Holy Spirit.

"Blessed are you among women, and blessed is the fruit of your womb!" Elizabeth said to Mary. "When the voice of your greeting came to my ears, the babe in my womb leaped for joy."

"My spirit rejoices in God my Savior," Mary said. "All generations will call me blessed; for he who is mighty has done great things for me, and holy is his name."

Mary stayed with her cousin Elizabeth, helping her for three months. At last, Elizabeth's baby, John, was born. Finally Zechariah was able to talk again! He went out and told everyone how wonderful and great God is.

WE ARE BLESSED WHEN WE OBEY GOD.

THE BIRTH OF JESUS: A KING IS BORN
(Luke 2:1-20)

It was almost time for Joseph and Mary's baby to be born, and their little home was ready. Joseph had made a cradle for the baby to sleep in. Mary had made some little clothes for the baby and some blankets to wrap him in.

But Mary and Joseph were sad. They had to go on a very long trip soon, and they were worried that the baby might be born before they returned home.

Their home was a part of the Roman Empire, a land ruled by a man named Caesar Augustus. Caesar wanted to take a census to count all the people he ruled. So everyone had to go to his or her hometown to be counted. Joseph and Mary were descendants of King David, so they had to go to Bethlehem to be counted. Sadly, they began their trip.

When Joseph and Mary got to Bethlehem, the town was crowded. Everyone was there for the census. Joseph and Mary were tired from their long trip, but there was no place for them to stay. All the inns were full. Finally, a kind innkeeper told Joseph that he and Mary could sleep in the stable where the animals stay. There was no bed, but there was clean hay to keep them warm

So Joseph and Mary went to the stable and made a bed in the sweet-smelling hay. There was a little wooden manger to hold the food for the animals. Joseph put some clean hay in the manger to make a little bed for the baby who would soon arrive.

That night Baby Jesus was born. Joseph and Mary wrapped him in soft blankets and put him to sleep in the manger. How strange that must have seemed. Here was a very special baby, a new little king, sleeping in the hay.

There were some shepherds out in the field that night with their sheep. An angel of God came to them. At first, the shepherds were frightened at the sight of this shining angel. But then the angel spoke to them:

"Be not afraid; for behold, I bring you good news of a great joy which will come to all the people; for to you is born this day in the city of David a Savior, who is Christ the Lord."

More angels joined the first angel, and they all began to sing a beautiful song of praise to God.

The shepherds were amazed and happy at the news. They went to the town of Bethlehem and searched in all the stables until they found a baby sleeping in a manger, just as the angel had said. They told Mary and Joseph about the angel's message. The shepherds knelt down and looked with love at the baby king. They thanked God for this blessing.

Mary remembered what the angel Gabriel had told her when he said she would have a baby. She kept the thoughts of these strange and wonderful happenings in her heart.

THE BIBLE TELLS US ABOUT GOD'S PROMISE TO SEND A NEW KING.

THREE KINGS: THE GIFTS OF THE MAGI
(Matthew 2:1-22)

In the lands of the East, there were three very wise men. They were called Magi, or kings. These men knew about the earth and the stars. They also knew about God's promise to send a new king.

One day, they saw a new star in the heavens. They knew this meant that the new king was born. They wanted to honor him, so they set out on a long journey. They followed the star, which led them to the land of Judah.

When the Magi neared Bethlehem, they began to ask where they could find the new king. Herod, the king of Judea, heard about this and grew very nervous. He wanted to be the only king of the land. Herod called these visitors from the East to him.

"Go and search diligently for the child, and when you have found him bring me word, that I too may come and worship him," Herod said.

But Herod was lying. He wanted to get rid of this new king. He hoped the Magi would help him find him.

The Magi continued to follow the new star. At last, it came to rest over the stable in Bethlehem. The richly dressed kings from the East knelt down in front of the manger to show their love for the new little king.

The Magi brought the baby gifts of gold, frankincense, and myrrh. Frankincense makes a beautiful smell when it is burned. Myrrh and gold were very expensive. These were gifts fit for a king.

That night the Magi had a strange dream. An angel told them not to go back to Herod, because he had lied and wanted to hurt Jesus. The Magi went home a different way without telling Herod where to find the baby.

Then Joseph had a dream. In his dream, an angel came to warn him about Herod and told him to leave Bethlehem. Joseph left with Mary and Baby Jesus that night. They escaped to Egypt, where they lived for several years.

When King Herod realized that the Magi had tricked him, he was very angry. Herod was jealous of the new little king. He told his soldiers to go kill all the children of Bethlehem younger than two years old, hoping that they would kill Baby Jesus. He didn't know the holy family had already escaped.

How the mothers and fathers of Bethlehem cried! Today we set aside a day, December 28, to remember these little children, called the Holy Innocents.

Finally, King Herod died. An angel came in a dream and told Joseph it was safe to go home. Joseph, Mary, and Baby Jesus could return to Nazareth at last.

The Bible does not list the names of these three wise men, but tradition tells us that the names of the Magi were Caspar, Melchior, and Balthasar.

THE PRESENTATION IN THE TEMPLE
(Luke 2:21-40)

Mary and Joseph were Jewish and faithfully followed the laws of the Jewish religion. One of these laws said that baby boys should be taken to the temple in Jerusalem to be presented there. Their parents had to bring a gift, or sacrifice, usually two birds. When the time came, Mary and Joseph took Baby Jesus to the temple.

There was an old man in Jerusalem named Simeon who loved God and prayed all his life. Because Simeon was so faithful, God had promised Simeon that he would not die until the Redeemer came to earth. The Holy Spirit led Simeon to the temple on the very same day that Mary and Joseph came to present Jesus.

When Simeon saw Jesus, his heart was full of joy. He knew that this baby was the Promised One sent by God. Simeon praised God and said, "Behold, this child is set for the fall and rising of many in Israel."

Then Simeon did a strange thing. He turned to Mary and said, "A sword will pierce through your own soul." Simeon was warning Mary that something would happen to make her very sad. He wanted her to be prepared for Jesus' death on the cross.

An old woman named Anna was also in the temple that day. She was a prophetess and could tell people what was going to happen in the future. When she saw Baby Jesus, she gave thanks to God. She told everyone in the temple that this baby was going to be the Redeemer for God's people.

Mary and Joseph were amazed at the things they heard. They thought about what Simeon and Anna said, and kept the words in their hearts.

Today, the Church sets aside a special day, February 2, to remember when Joseph and Mary took Baby Jesus to the temple. The feast is called the Presentation.

In some countries, people put new clothes on a little statue of Baby Jesus. They take the statue to the church and ask the priest to bless it. Then they take the statue home to remind them of the child Jesus.

JESUS' HOME AT NAZARETH

What was Jesus' home like? The Bible does not tell us much about the time when he was growing up. But scientists have learned much about the daily lives of the people who lived when Jesus did. We can imagine what it was like in his home from what scientists tell us about other homes.

Joseph worked hard to take care of Mary and Jesus. He played with Jesus, and later taught him how to be a carpenter, making furniture and other things out of wood. The Bible tells us that Jesus was good and obeyed his parents.

Jesus' house probably only had one room, with a cave at the back to store things in. It was made of stone, with a flat roof covered with stones and dirt. The floor was made of stone, too. Nazareth had many hills and was near the mountains.

In the morning, the family would get up and roll up their bedding. Joseph, Mary, and Jesus would start their day with a prayer, facing the temple of Jerusalem. The family was Jewish, so Joseph and Jesus would wear a special prayer shawl over their shoulders and two small boxes on their wrists and foreheads. The boxes were made of parchment, a kind of paper, and had the words to the prayer inside. At night, the family would say the same prayer to remind them that God would be with them as long as his people obeyed.

Next, the family would eat bread, fruit, and olives for breakfast, saying a blessing over their food. As Joseph and Jesus left for work, they would touch a little box on the door called a "mezuzah." This box also had a prayer inside. Then they would kiss their hands as a sign of respect for God and his promises.

Mary would wash the dishes and sweep the floor. Then she would put a shawl on her head and take a jug down to the fountain in the center of town to get water for the family. Sometimes she would wash the family's clothes in the same fountain.

Next, Mary would grind wheat between two flat stones to make bread and take it to a big oven in town. The family only had a small grill at home. Mary also took wool and flax and spun them into thread or yarn. Then she would take them to a man who would weave them into cloth.

At lunch, the family ate a big meal — bread, fruit, and meat or fish. They had wine to drink. In the evening, they had bread and vegetables or cheese.

After supper, Mary and Joseph would talk about God and teach Jesus the Law of Moses, the Psalms, and other stories of the Israelites. When it got dark, they would light a lamp, made with a piece of cloth or string in a dish of olive oil. After evening prayers, the family would unroll their bedding and go to sleep.

On Fridays, when the sun went down, Joseph and Jesus would go to the synagogue, a building where Jewish people pray. Each home would have a candle in the window and a special candleholder, called a "menorah," on the table.

Saturday was called the "Sabbath." On Saturday mornings, the family would go to the synagogue for a special service. At noon, they would go home to eat the meal Mary had made the day before. The Jews did not work, even to make dinner, on the Sabbath. In the afternoon, they would take a little walk before going back to the synagogue for the vesper service. The Sabbath ended when the sun went down. Then the children would play in the streets while the men visited and talked, and the women went to the fountain for water.

The holy family lived a simple, happy life in their little home in Nazareth.

Great Sea
(Mediterranean)

Cana   Capernaum   Bethsa

Nazareth

Sea of
Galilee

Mount Carmel   GALILEE

SAMARIA

DECAPOLIS

JUDEA

Jerusalem   Mount of   Jericho
Olives

Emmaus

Jordan River

PEREA

Bethany

Dead Sea

Bethlehem

JESUS IS FOUND IN THE TEMPLE
(Luke 2:41-52)

At his little home in Nazareth, Jesus grew tall and strong in spirit. God's grace was with him.

Each year Mary and Joseph went on a long trip, called a pilgrimage, to the temple in Jerusalem with the other Jews. When Jesus was twelve, he went with Joseph and Mary for the first time to celebrate the Passover there. At twelve, Jesus was nearly old enough to be a "Son of the Law," or a grown man.

A group of men, women, and children all traveled together to Jerusalem. Many were friends and relatives of Joseph and Mary. They talked and visited along the way, while the children played.

At last they reached the holy city. There were special services in the temple, and incense was burned to make a sweet smell while everyone worshiped God. Later, the holy family ate a special Passover meal of roasted lamb, bitter herbs, and unleavened bread to remind them of the Israelites' escape over the Red Sea from Egypt.

After three days, the ceremonies were over. The little group of pilgrims gathered their tents and began the trip back to Nazareth. Joseph did not see Jesus, but he thought the boy was with his mother. Mary did not see Jesus. She thought Jesus was with Joseph and the other men.

But where was Jesus? In the temple! He wandered around, watching what was going on. Jesus was so interested that he lost all track of time. He began to listen to a group of men who were teaching. At first he stood quietly, then he sat down and began to ask them questions.

That night, Joseph began to look for Jesus. Jesus was not with the men, so Joseph crossed to the women's camp to ask Mary if Jesus was with her. But he was not – Jesus was missing!

Joseph and Mary searched the entire camp, but they did not find Jesus. It was dark, so they lay down, praying to God that Jesus was safe. As soon as it was light, they got up and hurried back to Jerusalem.

Everywhere, they asked about Jesus. Mary and Joseph prayed to God for help in finding him. They were frantic and frightened.

Finally, after three days, Joseph and Mary came to the temple. There was Jesus! He was talking to the wise teachers.

Mary rushed up and hugged him. Then she said, "Son, why have you treated us so? Behold, your father and I have been looking for you anxiously."

Surprised, Jesus looked at his mother and said, "Did you not know that I must be in my Father's house?"

Joseph and Mary did not understand what Jesus meant. They did not realize that Jesus was talking about God, his Father in heaven.

Jesus went home with Joseph and Mary and obeyed them. Joseph and Mary were happy that Jesus was safe. They were glad that they had found little lost Jesus.

JOHN BAPTIZES JESUS
(Luke 3:1-22, Matthew 3, John 1:19-40)

John, the cousin of Jesus, lived in the countryside near the River Jordan. He began to tell people about God. He told them that they should be sorry for their sins, because God was soon going to send the Savior to make up for those sins. Those who were sorry went with John to the river, where he baptized them in the water. He was soon known as John the Baptist.

The people asked John whether he was the one God promised them, the one who would redeem God's people.

"I baptize you with water; but he who is mightier than I is coming," said John. "He will baptize you with the Holy Spirit and with fire."

They knew John was a great prophet, which means he could tell them about things that were going to happen. They wanted to be ready for the kingdom of heaven.

When Jesus was thirty years old, he went to the River Jordan to see his cousin John. Jesus asked John to baptize him, but John knew that Jesus was the Son of God, the one he had been preaching about. John was surprised. "I need to be baptized by you, and do you come to me?" John said.

But Jesus said, "Let it be so now."

So they walked into the river. John baptized Jesus with water. Suddenly, the heavens opened and the Holy Spirit, like a dove, came down and landed on Jesus' head! Then a loud voice from heaven said, "This is my beloved Son, with whom I am well pleased."

The people were amazed. They knew then that Jesus was the promised Redeemer, the one who would die to make up for their sins. Some of the people began to follow him and to listen to what he was teaching. Jesus told them to be sorry for their sins and to be more loving, because it was time for the kingdom of heaven to come to earth.

Jesus Calls the Apostles
(Matthew 4:18-22, 10:1-15)

Jesus went to the Sea of Galilee to preach. There he saw two fishermen, brothers named Peter and Andrew. Jesus called to them, saying "Follow me, and I will make you fishers of men." Peter and Andrew left their fishing right away and followed Jesus to help teach about God's love.

Next, Jesus saw two other brothers, James and John, in a boat with their father fixing their fishing nets. Again, Jesus called out and invited them to become fishers of men. He wanted them to help capture people's hearts with love for God. James and John also went with Jesus.

Many people began to follow Jesus around Galilee to hear him teach about God. Jesus knew he would need good friends to help spread his message, so he chose twelve men to go with him to learn about God and share his Good News. Peter, Andrew, James, and John were part of this group. Jesus also called Philip, Bartholomew, Matthew, Thomas, another man named James, Simon, Thaddeus, and Judas Iscariot. Jesus called these men his apostles.

Jesus sent the Twelve Apostles out to cure the sick and talk about the kingdom of God. He told them to take nothing with them on their trips. They had to trust God to give them what they needed on their journeys.

THE WEDDING AT CANA
(John 2:1-12)

Jesus and his family and friends were invited to a wedding at Cana, a town near his home in Galilee. There was a big meal, a feast for all the guests. During the celebration, Mary, Jesus' mother, heard that the bride and groom had run out of wine to drink. How embarrassing this would be! Mary told Jesus, "They have no wine." She wanted Jesus to help them.

Jesus tried to say no. He said it was not time yet to begin performing miracles.

But Mary knew that Jesus would help if she asked. She turned to the servants and said, "Do whatever he tells you."

Jesus told the servants to bring him some jars of water. Quickly, the servants filled six large stone jugs to the brim with water. Then Jesus told the man in charge of the feast to taste it. A miracle had happened! Jesus had turned the water into wine, even better than the wine they had served at the beginning of the wedding.

The wedding celebration was saved. When Jesus' apostles saw this miracle, they believed even more in his power.

JESUS TEACHES AND HEALS
(Matthew 5-7)

Everywhere Jesus went, people came to hear him. Many of those people were sick, and asked Jesus to make them well. Jesus healed many of them. He explained that their belief in God had made them better. Jesus told them to be happy and rejoice because of God's goodness.

One day, Jesus went up on a mountain to teach the people who came to hear him. Here on the mountain, Jesus preached a special sermon. He told the people to be kind and good to everyone, even their enemies. Jesus told them to make peace with people who hurt them. He said those who love God are the light of the world, and that they must let that light shine. He told them God is love, and that they should rely on God to take care of them.

Then Jesus told the people about nine special blessings. We call these the Beatitudes. These blessings of Jesus are like promises for us.

"**Blessed are those who realize the need for the Lord in their lives**, for theirs is the kingdom of heaven."

"**Blessed are those who mourn**, for they shall be comforted."

"**Blessed are the meek**, for they shall inherit the earth."

"**Blessed are those who hunger and thirst for righteousness**, for they shall be satisfied."

"**Blessed are the merciful**, for they shall obtain mercy."

"**Blessed are the pure in heart**, for they shall see God."

"**Blessed are the peacemakers**, for they shall be called sons of God."

"**Blessed are those who are persecuted for righteousness' sake**, for theirs is the kingdom of heaven."

"**Blessed are you when men revile you and persecute you and utter all kinds of evil against you falsely on my account.** Rejoice and be glad, for your reward is great in heaven."

— Matthew 5:1-12

LOAVES AND FISHES
(John 6:1-14, Matthew 14:15-21)

JESUS TAUGHT CROWDS OF PEOPLE ABOUT SPECIAL BLESSINGS.

Crowds of people had been listening to Jesus teach all day near the Sea of Galilee. It was almost time for dinner, and everyone was growing very hungry. Jesus pointed this out to his friends, the apostles.

"How are we to buy bread, so that these people may eat?" Jesus asked Philip. Philip replied that they didn't have the money to buy enough food for everyone to have even a little. But Jesus had a plan.

Andrew told Jesus there was a boy in the crowd who had five barley loaves and two fish. "But what are they among so many?" Andrew asked. He didn't think that little bit would make any difference.

Jesus smiled and told his apostles to ask everyone to have a seat. Then Jesus took the two fish and the five loaves of bread and looked up to heaven. He blessed the food and told the apostles to begin feeding the people.

Because they believed in him, the apostles did as Jesus asked. They were surprised to see there was enough to feed everyone in the crowd as much as they wanted. There was even enough left over to fill twelve baskets. It was a miracle!

When the people saw this, they said, "This is indeed the prophet who is to come into the world."

JESUS LOVES CHILDREN
(Luke 18:15-18)

Everywhere Jesus went, he attracted large crowds of people who wanted to hear him teach, ask him to cure their illnesses, or receive a blessing.

One day when Jesus was speaking, a group of mothers brought their children to him to be blessed. But the apostles told them to leave. Jesus was too busy with the adults, they said, and didn't have time for children.

When Jesus heard this, he was very unhappy with his friends. "Let the children come to me," he said, "for to such belongs the kingdom of God."

Jesus hugged and held the children. He put his hands on their heads and blessed them. The children knew Jesus loved them very much.

Jesus told the crowd: "Truly, I say to you, whoever does not receive the kingdom of God like a child shall not enter it." Jesus reminded the adults that they were all children of God, and that they must obey and love their Heavenly Father.

THE STORIES OF JESUS

Jesus was a wonderful teacher. Instead of telling people what to do, he told them stories. These stories made his lessons easy to understand and remember. We call Jesus' stories "parables."

Each parable has a message about how God wants us to live. The following are a few of Jesus' stories. There are many more great parables in your Bible.

THE PARABLE OF THE SEEDS
(Luke 8:4-18)

A farmer went out to plant some seed. As he was throwing the seeds on the ground, some fell onto the path and were eaten by birds. Some of the seeds fell on rocks and dried up in the sun. Some of the seeds fell into a patch of weeds and died in the shade. But some of the seeds fell on good ground. Those plants grew tall and strong and had plenty of fruit.

Jesus said his words are like the seeds. Is our heart like the bad ground, where the seeds of Jesus' message will die? Or is our heart like the good soil, where his words of love can grow?

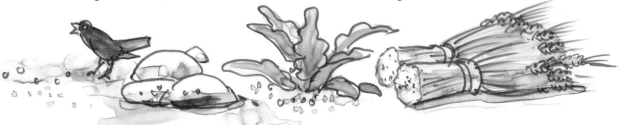

THE PARABLE OF THE MUSTARD SEED
(Luke 13:18-19)

Jesus' listeners asked him to explain what the kingdom of heaven is like. Jesus said it is like a mustard seed – it starts out very, very small, but if it is planted in good ground, it will grow big enough for birds to make their nests in.

The Unforgiving Servant
(Matthew 18:21-35)

One day a king sat counting how much his servants owed him. The king called in one servant who owed him a huge amount, and told the servant he and all of his things would be sold to pay off the money.

The servant cried and fell on his knees in front of the king. "Have patience with me, and I will pay you everything," he said to the king.

The king felt sorry for the servant. He told him he would not have to pay his debt.

A few days later, that same servant went to one of his co-workers who owed him some money. "Pay what you owe," he said angrily.

The fellow servant fell down on his knees and said, "Have patience with me, and I will pay you."

But the man would not listen. He had his fellow servant thrown in jail.

The king was furious. "You wicked servant!" he said. "Should not you have had mercy on your fellow servant, as I had mercy on you?" He punished the servant.

Jesus said God is like the patient king; he will forgive us, but we must forgive others, too.

THE GOOD SHEPHERD
(Luke 15:1-7)

The people in charge of the government couldn't understand why Jesus spent time with sinners and people who collect taxes. They asked him why he would waste his time with those bad people. Jesus answered them with a parable.

A shepherd will leave his ninety-nine sheep alone in the desert to go looking for one lost sheep, Jesus said. "And when he has found it, he lays it on his shoulders, rejoicing. And when he comes home, he calls together his friends and his neighbors, saying to them, 'Rejoice with me, for I have found my sheep.'"

It is the same when one of God's people is lost because of sin, Jesus said. Like a good shepherd, Jesus watches those who are safe in God's love, but goes to bring back a lost sinner. When a sinner is saved, there is great joy in heaven, he said.

THE GREATEST COMMANDMENT
(Matthew 22:34-40)

The people knew that God had given Moses the Ten Commandments for them to live by. They asked Jesus which was the greatest commandment of all.

He said to them, "'You shall love the Lord your God with all your heart, and with all your soul, and with all your mind.' This is the great and first commandment. And a second is like it, 'You shall love your neighbor as yourself.' On these two commandments depend all the law and the prophets."

JESUS TELLS US HOW WE SHOULD LIVE.

THE LAST SUPPER: JESUS SAYS GOODBYE
(Luke 22:1-39, John 13-17, Matthew 26:14-30, Mark 14:12-26)

Jesus knew God was going to call him soon to die on the cross. Jesus gathered his friends together for one last supper. He wanted to prepare the apostles for the frightening days ahead.

The friends enjoyed a good meal. While they were eating, Jesus took some bread and blessed it. He broke it into pieces and gave it to his disciples. He told them, "Take, eat; this is my body."

Then Jesus took the cup of wine, gave thanks to God, and blessed it. He said, "This is my blood of the covenant, which is poured out for many for the forgiveness of sins."

Jesus told his apostles that after he went home to heaven, they should turn bread and wine into his Body and Blood and give it to his people. "Do this in remembrance of me," he said.

After supper, Jesus knelt down and washed the apostles' feet. He wanted to show his love and to remind them how important it is to take care of one another.

Jesus knew there was one apostle at dinner that night who did not really love him. Jesus knew Judas Iscariot would tell the soldiers where to find him when they wanted to kill him. Jesus told Judas to go and do what he needed to do. The other apostles did not understand where Judas was going. But Jesus knew that Judas' betrayal was part of God's plan.

Jesus told his friends that he would be leaving them soon. He talked to them about how to keep spreading God's message after he was gone. But Jesus promised his friends he would come back and see them again. Then he and his apostles went out into a little garden to pray.

While the others were praying, Judas hurried off to make a deal. The soldiers and the government were going to pay Judas money so he would tell them where Jesus was.

JESUS DIES ON THE CROSS
(John 18-19, Luke 22-23, Matthew 27, Mark 15)

Jesus prayed in a garden after his last supper with his friends, the apostles. He told God that he hoped he might not have to die on the cross, but that he would do whatever God wanted.

Soon the Roman soldiers came to the garden and took Jesus prisoner. They took him to the chief priest, who asked Jesus if he thought he was the Son of God. Jesus said, "You say that I am." Others who had heard Jesus preaching said that Jesus called God his Father. This was against the law. The chief priest said Jesus was guilty and would have to die. The people spit on him and hit him. They took him to the Roman governor, Pontius Pilate.

Pilate asked Jesus, "Are you the king of the Jews?" But Jesus only said, "You have said so."

Pilate said Jesus was not guilty. He asked the people whether he should let Jesus go, or let Barabbas, a murderer, out of jail. The people shouted that he should let Barabbas go and hang Jesus on the cross instead. Pilate said that Jesus was innocent, but the crowds kept shouting, "Crucify him!"

Pilate handed Jesus over to the soldiers, who beat him and made fun of him for preaching about the kingdom of heaven. They put a crown of thorns on his head. They put a sign on the cross that said, "Jesus of Nazareth, the King of the Jews."

The soldiers made Jesus carry his cross to the hill called Golgotha, where he would be crucified. The wooden cross was huge and very heavy, and Jesus fell three times while he carried it. The soldiers grabbed a nearby traveler named Simon and made him help Jesus. Veronica, a kind woman by the side of the road, wiped Jesus' face with her handkerchief.

At Golgotha, the soldiers made Jesus lie down on the cross and nailed him to it. Then they raised up the cross and waited for Jesus to die.

Jesus' mother, Mary, and one of his friends, John, were standing nearby. Jesus asked John to care for his mother, who was brokenhearted.

Jesus looked up to heaven and said, "Father, forgive them, for they know not what they do."

That same day, the soldiers crucified two thieves, one on each side of Jesus.

One of them was angry. Looking at Jesus, he said, "Are you not the Christ? Save yourself and us!" But the other thief said, "This man has done nothing wrong…. Jesus, remember me when you come into your kingdom." Jesus told the second man, "Today you will be with me in Paradise."

At last, Jesus breathed his last breath and said, "It is finished."

Suddenly there was a loud clap of thunder, and the curtain in the temple tore apart. The crowd was afraid and worried about what they had done.

Later that day, some friends of Jesus took his body off the cross, carefully wrapped it, and laid it in a tomb, a cave carved out of rock. A huge stone was rolled in front of the opening. After staying there a while, Jesus' sad friends went home.

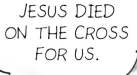

JESUS DIED ON THE CROSS FOR US.

Jesus Is Alive!
(Luke 24)

How sad Jesus' friends were after his death!

Two days later, on Sunday morning, some of the women went to Jesus' tomb. When they got there, they discovered that the huge stone blocking the entrance to the tomb had been rolled away. They looked inside, but the body of Jesus was gone.

Suddenly two angels appeared. The women were frightened and bowed down. The angels said, "Why do you seek the living among the dead?" Jesus was risen, they told the women.

The women ran back to tell the apostles the good news. Not all of Jesus' friends believed them. But Peter went to the tomb and was amazed to see that Jesus' body was gone.

That same day, two of Jesus' friends were walking to a town called Emmaus. Suddenly, a man joined them on their walk. It was Jesus! But they did not recognize him. Jesus talked to them about the Scriptures during their journey, and when they got to Emmaus, the two apostles asked Jesus to stay with them. During supper, Jesus took some bread and wine and blessed it. Finally, the two apostles recognized Jesus!

With that, Jesus disappeared. The two friends ran back to Jerusalem where the other disciples were gathered and told them the good news. While they were talking, Jesus appeared again. The other disciples were frightened and thought he was a ghost.

"Why are you troubled?" said Jesus. Then he showed them the marks of the nails in his hands and feet. They were overjoyed to see it was really Jesus, alive.

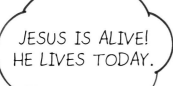

JESUS IS ALIVE! HE LIVES TODAY.

Jesus explained that everything happened just the way God planned it. "I send the promise of my Father upon you; but stay in the city, until you are clothed with power from on high," he said.

Then Jesus and his friends walked to Bethany. After he blessed the apostles, Jesus was suddenly lifted to heaven. The apostles were amazed and happy. They went back to Jerusalem praising God.

PENTECOST: THE HOLY SPIRIT COMES
(Acts 1-2)

When Jesus came to see the apostles after he rose from the dead, he promised that God would send the Holy Spirit to his friends with a special gift. He told the apostles and Mary to go to Jerusalem to wait for the coming of the Spirit. Jesus then ascended into heaven, rising on a cloud to be with his Father.

The apostles and Mary went to Jerusalem, praying to God and praising him. They were gathered together when they heard a strong wind. The sound rushed in the windows and filled the house. Then a light that looked like a flame appeared over the heads of Mary and each of Jesus' friends. They were filled with the Holy Spirit, and each started to speak in a different language.

Many people in town heard the loud wind. They came running to see what was happening. The people in this crowd were from many different faraway places, but each heard Jesus' friends speaking in his own different language. They were amazed. The apostles were talking about the wonderful power of God.

"What does this mean?" shouted a man in the crowd.

Peter told the crowd that even though Jesus had died on the cross, he had come back to life. He told the people that God wanted everyone to be sorry for their sins and to be baptized in the name of Jesus. He told the people that they could be filled with the Holy Spirit, too.

That very day about three thousand people were baptized. The apostles knew it was time for them to go out into the world and spread the Good News about Jesus. They would tell everyone that Jesus died for them, so their sins will be forgiven and they can live with him in heaven.

MARY, OUR BEAUTIFUL QUEEN: THE ASSUMPTION

When Jesus died on the cross, he asked his friend John to take care of his mother, Mary. Jesus also told his mother that John would be like a son to her.

John was with Mary when her life on this earth ended. She told John goodbye, and he suddenly saw a beautiful vision. John saw a sign in heaven – a woman wearing the sun, with the moon under her feet. She had a crown of twelve stars. John knew that Jesus had something special in mind for his mother.

On Mary's last day on earth, Jesus brought her, body and soul, into heaven. Here she reigns over all the saints as a queen. We celebrate the day that Mary was assumed into heaven on August 15, the Feast of the Assumption. Because her son, Jesus, is the King of Heaven, we call Mary our beautiful Queen of Heaven.

Mary has many other names, or titles. We call her Our Lady, Our Mother, Holy Queen, and many other beautiful phrases. She is the same Mary, no matter what title we call her.

Mary is the most special woman who ever lived. She was born without the stain of Adam and Eve's sin on her soul. Because she was born with no stain of sin, one of the names we call her is the Immaculate Conception. This means that her soul was always pure and clean, even from the time she was born.

Just as Mary was the Mother of Jesus, we call her our mother, too. She knows her son wants all of us to come and live with him in heaven one day. She wants to help us know and love Jesus. She wants to bring us to the King. We pray to Mary and ask her to bring us close to Jesus.

III.
THE CHURCH BEGINS TO GROW

YOU CAN BE A DISCIPLE OF GOD!

When the Holy Spirit came on Pentecost, Jesus' friends, the apostles, knew that they must become brave missionaries. They would go out into the world to tell the Good News about Jesus.

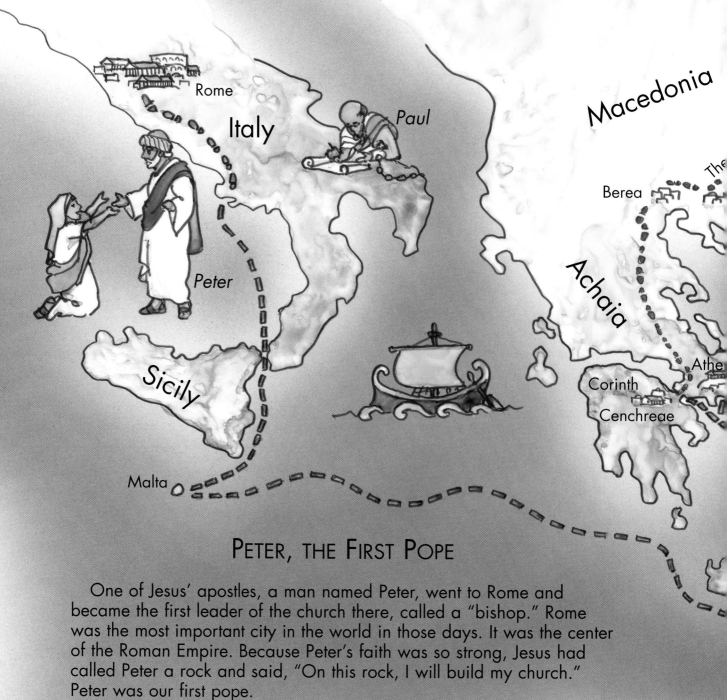

PETER, THE FIRST POPE

One of Jesus' apostles, a man named Peter, went to Rome and became the first leader of the church there, called a "bishop." Rome was the most important city in the world in those days. It was the center of the Roman Empire. Because Peter's faith was so strong, Jesus had called Peter a rock and said, "On this rock, I will build my church." Peter was our first pope.

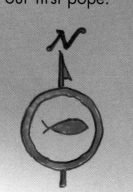

PAUL TELLS EVERYONE

At first, all of Jesus' friends were members of the Jewish religion. Some of these apostles felt nervous about preaching to people who were not Jews, called "Gentiles." But Paul said that Jesus had died to save everyone, not just one group.

Paul began to travel from city to city. Whenever he found people who believed the Good News about Jesus, Paul started a church. Soon these believers began to call themselves "Christians," because they followed Christ. Paul wrote many long letters, called "epistles," to the Christians in the new churches, telling them how to live as Jesus wanted them to live.

Philippi

Troas

Asia

Paul and Timothy

Ephesus

Pisidian Antioch

Iconium

Derbe

Perga

Attalia

Tarsus

Patara

Myra

Antioch

SPREADING THE NEWS AROUND THE WORLD

Cyprus

Salamis

Paphos

Syria

te

Other friends of Jesus went to the East, to important cities such as Alexandria and Antioch. Some of the apostles even went to cities outside the Roman Empire to begin churches in Persia and Germany.

At first, the apostles spread the Good News alone. But many new Christians wanted to be missionaries, too, helping share God's Word. We have a special name for those people who try to live the way Jesus taught us; we call them "disciples." The apostles and disciples wanted everyone to change from their old ways and convert to Christianity. The disciples were happy to tell other people about their friend Jesus and the way he taught them to love each other.

Tyre

Ptolemais

Jerusalem

Alexandria

Egypt

Judea

IV.

THE CHURCH COVERS EUROPE

THE SAINTS OF EUROPE

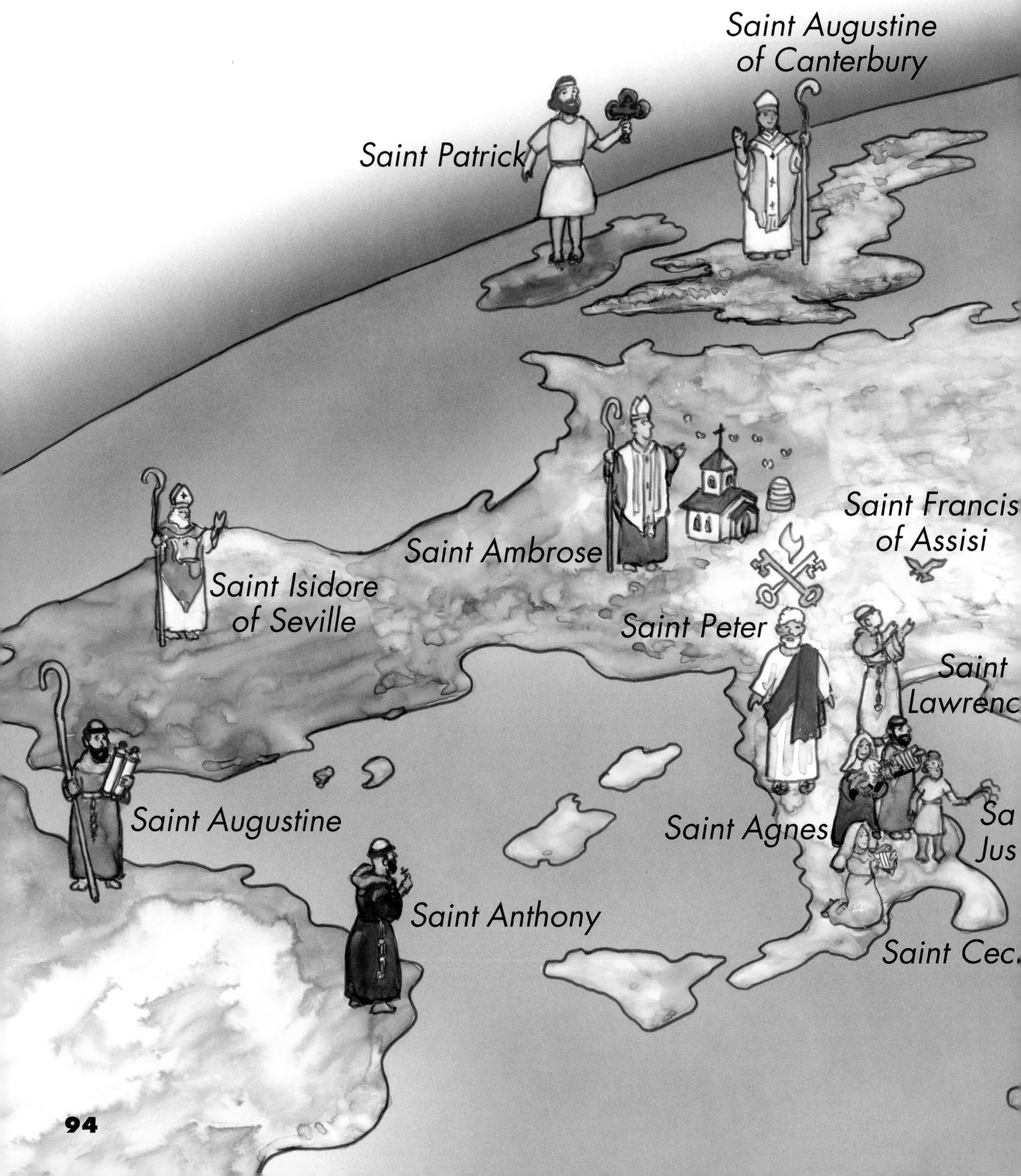

Saint Augustine
of Canterbury

Saint Patrick

Saint Ambrose

Saint Francis
of Assisi

Saint Isidore
of Seville

Saint Peter

Saint
Lawrenc

Saint Augustine

Saint
Jus

Saint Agnes

Saint Anthony

Saint Cec.

Saint Boniface

Saint Cyril

Saint Methodius

Constantine

Saint Helena

Saint Jerome

CHRISTIANS IN DANGER:
THE EARLY CHURCH AND PERSECUTION

For about two hundred fifty years, Christians lived in fear and danger. The Romans worshiped false gods. But the Christians refused to worship these gods. They only wanted to worship the one true God that Jesus taught us about.

Sometimes the Romans ignored the Christians. Other times, the Romans punished them for not worshiping the Roman gods. They beat the Christians, or sold them as slaves. Sometimes they killed them by feeding them to hungry lions or cutting off their heads.

The Christians who were killed for being faithful to the one true God are called martyrs. They died for their beliefs. As a reward for being faithful, God took them straight to heaven. Saints Cecilia, Agnes, Justin, and Lawrence were all brave young Christian martyrs. They were heroes, and even today we remember their names at Mass.

Christians had suffered for many years when a man named Constantine became the emperor of Rome. One day before a big battle, Constantine saw a cross in the sky. There was a message on the cross telling Constantine that he would win the battle because of the cross. The message said: "In this sign, you will conquer." After his victory, Constantine became a Christian. He and his friend Licinius agreed that all religions would be respected in the Roman Empire. There would be no more persecution of the Christians.

Constantine helped the Church in many ways. He gathered the bishops for a meeting, and they wrote down what the Christians believe. Their list is called the Nicene Creed. We say it during Mass on Sundays.

Constantine gave money to the Christians so they could build many churches. His mother, Helena, went to the Holy Land and found the Holy Cross of Jesus. She built a church in Jerusalem for this precious relic, or reminder, of Jesus. She found many other holy relics, items from Jesus' time on earth, and brought them to Rome so Christians would have them as precious keepsakes of Our Lord.

IN HOC SIGNO VINCES

CHRISTIANS DEVOTE THEIR LIVES TO JESUS

As Christian missionaries traveled through Europe in the three hundred years after Jesus' return to heaven, they persuaded many people to follow Jesus and join the Christian faith. Other Christians wrote letters and books to explain the Christian faith to people called pagans, who believed in false gods. Today we call these Christian writers "Doctors of the Church" and "Church Fathers."

Some people who said they were Christians began to change Jesus' teachings. Those people are called "heretics." But the Doctors of the Church and the Church Fathers taught people the true meaning of Jesus' teachings. It was their job to give the correct answers when people asked about the faith. Saint Augustine, Saint Jerome, and Saint Ambrose were three writers who helped spread the truth about Jesus. Some of the books they wrote are still read today.

Saint Anthony was another holy man. When people punished the Christians for following Jesus, Saint Anthony went into the desert to devote his entire life to God. Other men soon joined Saint Anthony in a life of prayer. They wanted Saint Anthony to teach them how to be holy. We call these men "monks." The monks built a large home called a "monastery." They spent many hours there praying.

Some women wanted to live a holy life of prayer like the monks. They, too, built a large house, called an "abbey," where they could live and pray together. We call these women "nuns."

THE MIDDLE AGES: THE AGE OF FAITH

The years from about 450 to about 1450 are known as the Middle Ages, or the Age of Faith.

During this time, the Church helped keep things peaceful. The missionaries were preaching and converting people to Christianity. The monks copied books to save ancient stories.

During the Middle Ages, armies from the northern part of Europe often attacked cities in the rest of Europe. After a while, the western part of the Roman Empire couldn't fight back anymore. Kings and great warriors, called "knights," tried to protect the people in the Roman Empire, but the attackers destroyed many of the great cities built by the Romans.

Soon, the kings and the knights worked with leaders called "nobles" to build strong castles to protect themselves from the attackers. The kings and nobles were very rich and owned all the land. Their castles and the lands around them became known as "manors."

Men called "serfs" worked for the kings and nobles. They were poor and did not own any land. The serfs grew crops on land they borrowed from the kings and nobles. When they harvested the crops, the serfs gave half to the king or noble who owned the land. The serfs were not allowed to leave the manor. They lived in small towns near the castle, hoping that the powerful knights would keep them safe.

Other men were known as "freemen." They were allowed to leave the manor. Many of these freemen learned how to make and repair things, such as furniture and tools. The freemen sold the things they made in the towns' shops.

The most important job of the Church in the Middle Ages was to help men save their souls. But things were often very hard for the serfs and freemen, so the Church also helped men have a better life on earth. The Church started schools, took care of the poor and the sick, built hospitals, and set up homes for people who had no place to stay. The Church also encouraged peace. If a man ran into a church building, he would be safe from his enemies. No fighting was allowed in a church.

SAINT BENEDICT'S MONASTERY: A LIFE OF PRAYER

Monks are groups of men who join together to give their lives to God. Most monks live very quiet lives. One of these men, Saint Benedict, became famous when he created a rule for how to live a holy life.

Benedict gathered a group of men and started a monastery, a place where the monks could live and pray together. Then in about the year 530, Benedict came up with a rule for the monks. He said they should live in a monastery and spend all their time working and praying to God. The monks promised to be poor, to obey the abbot who was in charge of the monastery, and to never get married. Word of Benedict's rule spread, and soon monasteries all over Europe began to follow it.

Some of the monks were priests, and those monks who were not priests were called "brothers." The monks shaved their heads as a sign that their life was given to God. They wore a wool outfit called a habit, and a long apron called a scapular.

Seven times a day, a large bell rang at the monastery, and the monks went into the church to praise God. The rest of the day, they worked without talking. The monks built their own buildings, grew their own food, and made all the things they needed.

In those days there were no hotels, so the monastery built a small house where travelers could rest. Some monks taught the farmers better ways to raise crops and care for their animals. Other monks were scribes, carefully copying books by hand on pieces of parchment and painting beautiful pictures on the borders of the pages. The monastery had a library where these treasures were kept.

Some monks grew an herb garden. There were no doctors nearby, so the monks planted herbs that could be used as medicine. The monastery set aside space for a small hospital, and the monks cared for the sick there.

The monks helped the people of their community in many ways and offered many prayers to God.

A Medieval Town

Manor

Shops

King

Knight

Hospital

Cloister

Serfs' Huts

Serf

Cells

Monks

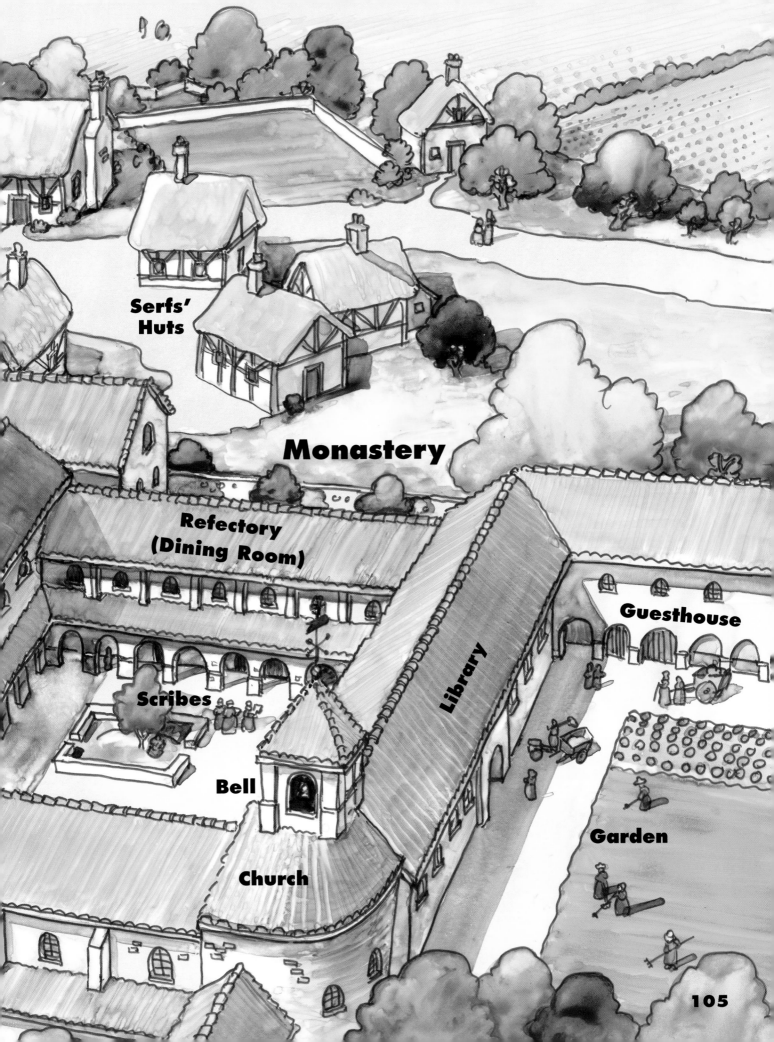

Serfs' Huts

Monastery

Refectory (Dining Room)

Guesthouse

Scribes

Library

Bell

Garden

Church

SAINT FRANCIS AND HIS CHRISTMAS SURPRISE

Saint Francis of Assisi was the best-loved holy man in the Middle Ages. He loved God and others so much that he was named a saint right after his death.

Francis wasn't always so good. He was born in Assisi, Italy, the son of a rich merchant. When Francis was a young man, he lived a sinful life. He made some bad friends and wasted his father's money. But suddenly the Holy Spirit came to him, and he decided to serve God by helping the sick and poor.

Though he was rich, Francis gave away everything he owned. He wore an old brown robe and went from town to town telling people of God's love. He called everyone his brothers and sisters, even the animals. He always tried to help other people.

Soon other people were so impressed by Francis and what he had to say that they joined him in his work. Today we call Francis' followers the "Franciscans."

When Francis was alive, it was a tradition at Christmastime to make a long trip, called a "pilgrimage," to the Holy Land to see the places where Jesus had lived and preached. Francis knew that most people could not afford to leave their homes and jobs to make such a long trip, though, so he planned a big surprise. The brothers who had joined Francis in his work helped him set up the surprise.

When people came to church on Christmas Eve of 1223, they couldn't believe their eyes. There, in front of the church, was a stable with cows and a donkey. A man and woman were standing by a manger, and a baby was asleep in the hay. Some shepherds and their sheep were near the stable. The shepherds were kneeling in prayer.

Francis preached a beautiful sermon. He told the people how our Lord Jesus Christ had come down from heaven and was born in a poor stable to show his love for us. The manger scene helped the people feel as if they had been to see the place where Jesus was born.

Even today many people put up a manger scene in their homes or churches at Christmas to remind them of how Jesus was born.

THE CRUSADES

Palestine was a place very important to the Christians, because Jesus had lived there. Many Christians from the West made trips called "pilgrimages" to the eastern part of the Roman Empire to worship Jesus.

But some people who were not Christians took over Palestine around the year 640. These new rulers would not let the pilgrims visit the holy places.

So the pope, some kings, and many brave knights decided to go to the East and take back the Holy Land. Some of these trips, called crusades, were successful. The Christians took charge of parts of the Holy Land.

But around the year 1290, the last crusaders gave up and went home. The Christians and the non-Christians made a deal: The Christians could visit the Holy Land, but they could not own it.

During these crusades to the Holy Land, the Christian armies marched through many large cities built by the Romans. They saw wonderful things they did not have at home, such as spices, beautiful rugs, and perfume and incense.

The crusaders took some of these things home with them, and people in the West loved them so much that they wanted to buy more. Some people realized they could make money by selling new things from faraway places. Fabrics, spices, and other treasures were traded from area to area. All this travel caused small towns to grow bigger.

MICHELANGELO AND THE SISTINE CHAPEL

Pope Julius II had hired the great artist Michelangelo to paint the walls of the Sistine Chapel in Rome. He wanted to make it the most beautiful chapel in the city. For four years, the artist worked and worked on the project. Surely he was nearly finished, the pope thought.

But Michelangelo had not been working on the walls. The artist decided to create his paintings in a different way. Michelangelo was lying on his back on top of a tall scaffold, like a ladder, at the top of the chapel. There, the entire ceiling was covered with beautiful pictures of scenes from the Bible!

People traveled from far away to see the amazing work. Today, nearly five hundred years later, people can still see Michelangelo's wonderful paintings on the ceiling of the Sistine Chapel.

Toward the end of the Middle Ages, many other exciting things began to happen in Western Europe. Learning and studying became very important. Artists painted many beautiful pictures, and scientists made great discoveries. Explorers began to travel the oceans. We call this time in the fourteenth through seventeenth centuries the Renaissance, which means "waking up" or "rebirth." The people began to wake up to the world around them.

MANY BIBLES COULD BE PRINTED WITH MOVEABLE TYPE.

A MOST WONDERFUL INVENTION

During the Renaissance, in the fourteenth through seventeenth centuries, many people made exciting discoveries and remarkable inventions. One very important invention in particular made it possible for you to read this book today.

The monks in the monasteries at that time made copies of books by writing out each page, a long, slow process. This meant there were very few books, and each was precious. Only the very rich could afford to buy a book.

But in about 1100, some men in Europe decided to try carving the words and pictures for a book on wooden blocks. The words were all carved backwards. The men then coated those blocks with ink and put a sheet of paper over the ink. When they lifted the paper off the ink, the words and pictures were printed on it. When blocks had been carved for every page, many copies of a book could be made, much more quickly than the monks could write them by hand.

The Chinese first printed from blocks like this for many years before the Europeans learned the process. They also knew how to make moveable type. To make moveable type, each letter of the alphabet is carved on its own block. The blocks can then be moved around to spell new words. In about 1450, Johannes Gutenberg, a German, printed a Bible using moveable type. This made printing even faster and less expensive. More and more people could afford to own books. More people began to learn to read. Knowledge – and copies of the Bible – began to spread rapidly.

Other important inventions during the Renaissance are things we still use today. The telescope helped astronomers, people who study the planets and stars, to see into the heavens. The invention of the microscope let scientists view, for the first time, the tiny creatures that live in the water around us. People began to measure things in new and better ways. Thermometers help us measure how cold or hot something is. Clocks help us measure time. As the years passed, the inventions were improved. Look at the pictures. Do the inventions of the Renaissance look like the things we use today?

THE REFORMATION: CHRISTIANS ARE DIVIDED

During the Middle Ages, the Catholic Church was the only Church in Western Europe.

But when more and more people learned how to read, they had new ideas. They also started to ask questions about what the Church taught. The Church began to have many problems. For a while, three different men each said they were the pope. There were many arguments.

A German priest named Martin Luther began to say things were wrong in the Church. The pope said Martin was not right and told him to stop saying those things. But Martin did not stop. The pope said Martin could no longer be a part of the Catholic Church, so Martin started a new church, and his followers were called "Lutherans." Other men saw what was happening and started their own churches. How sad God must have been to see his people fighting among themselves!

In 1545, the pope called a big meeting, called a "council," at Trent. The council worked for almost twenty years. They wanted to make the Catholic Church's lessons easier to understand, and they wanted to end problems in the Church. Many great saints helped the Church change and grow strong again. We call this time the "Reformation," because the church was trying to reform, or fix, its problems.

Other Christians have left the Catholic Church to start their own churches. They honor God in different ways. Although we do not believe the same things these people do, we show respect for their beliefs, because Christ taught us to love everyone. As Catholics, we pray that one day all Christians will be one big family again.

Blessed Kateri

Saint Frances Cabrini

V.

THE CHURCH IN THE NEW WORLD

Saint Martin de Porres

THE CHURCH CROSSES THE OCEAN

The people of Europe learned about the treasures in the faraway lands of the East during the crusades. Some missionaries and people who buy and sell things had gone to the East and returned with exciting stories and wonderful things.

Many explorers wanted to go to the East. The only way they knew how to get there, though, was to sail the ocean, then make a long, hard trip over land. But Prince Henry of Portugal and Vasco de Gama proved them wrong. They sailed south around Africa all the way to the lands of the East and brought back riches.

Christopher Columbus was a young boy who also dreamed of sailing away on a big boat to find spices, silk, and other riches. He worked with his father weaving wool in the great seaport of Genoa, where all the boats came in. As Christopher combed out the wool, his mind was on other things. He had heard the sailors talking about exciting places, and he wanted to go.

When Christopher was only fourteen, he got his wish and began making voyages, or trips, on a big ship. Between voyages, he learned how to make maps and studied geography.

When Christopher was twenty-six, he married the daughter of a famous ship captain from Portugal. He still studied maps and read about the great explorers. Christopher had an idea. He believed he could sail west around the world to get to the East. He didn't know how big the world was. What a different idea!

Christopher asked everyone to help him make his dream come true. He needed money to buy big boats to make the voyage. He even asked the king and queen of Spain.

King Ferdinand and Queen Isabella agreed to help Christopher. They gave him three boats. Away Christopher sailed to find the rich lands of the East and bring back spices, silk, and other treasures for Spain.

FLORIDA

San Salvador

CUBA

HISPAÑOLA

MEXICO

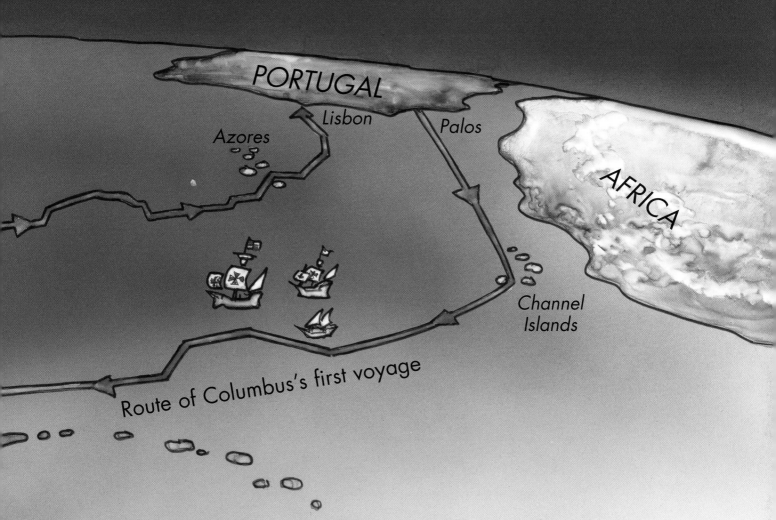

PORTUGAL

Lisbon

Azores

Palos

AFRICA

Channel
Islands

Route of Columbus's first voyage

Christopher sailed ... and sailed ... and sailed. Many of the other sailors on his boats thought they would never get there. Christopher's first voyage had taken him 224 days – almost a year! At last a happy sailor shouted, "Land!"

But Christopher had not reached the East. Instead, he landed on one of the Bahama Islands near Florida. He named it San Salvador, which means "Holy Savior" in Spanish. Christopher thought he had found the East Indies, so he called the friendly people of the island Indians.

Christopher left some of his men there to make a town while he sailed back to Spain with gold, parrots, strange plants, and several of the Indians. King Ferdinand and Queen Isabella were delighted! Christopher's different idea turned out to be a good one after all.

Christopher sailed again, three times. Queen Isabella asked him to take a priest along the second time so the Indians could hear the Good News about Jesus. The first Mass on the American continent was held on August 14, 1502, at a place that is now part of the country of Honduras.

SAINT JUAN DIEGO AND THE BEAUTIFUL LADY

Juan Diego was a poor working man who lived near Tepeyac in Mexico. Early one morning in December of 1531, he was walking to Mass when he heard some beautiful music and a sweet voice calling to him from the top of the nearby mountain. Juan Diego hurried to find out who it was.

At the top he saw a beautiful lady, with clothes as bright as the sun. She spoke to Juan Diego and gave him a job to do: She asked him to tell the bishop to build a church on the mountain, so that all the Indians could come to honor her as Mother of God and to worship her Son.

Juan walked to Mexico City to give the message to the bishop, a good and holy man. When the bishop heard Juan's story, he thought Juan was just imagining things. The bishop would not build a church. Sadly, Juan Diego began the long walk home.

When he reached the mountain, Juan saw the beautiful lady again. He told the woman he had failed to do what she had asked. She told him to try again the next day.

Juan made the long walk to the home of the bishop again the next day. This time the bishop told him to prove that the lady was really the Mother of God. Again, Juan Diego walked sadly home.

The beautiful woman told Juan to return in the morning. She said she would give him something that would prove to the bishop that he was not imagining things.

The next morning, Juan Diego's uncle was very sick. Juan hurried on the road to Mexico City to find a doctor. He went around the mountain to avoid seeing the woman. He had no time — he had to bring a doctor for his uncle. But as he came around the mountain, the lady was there. Juan Diego was embarrassed. He told the lady that he had to find a doctor and could not see the bishop that day.

The beautiful woman told Juan not to worry. His uncle would be cured. Then she told Juan to go to the top of the mountain and gather the roses growing there. Juan was surprised, because it was winter and too cold for roses, but he trusted and obeyed the beautiful lady. When he reached the top, he found it was true — there were many roses there. He picked some and carried them back to the lady.

The lady put the roses in Juan's overcoat, called a "tilma," She tied the ends of the cloak at the shoulder and told Juan not to open it until he was with the bishop. Juan ran to Mexico City to see him.

Juan told the bishop the story of the beautiful woman and the roses. Then he opened his cloak.

Immediately, the bishop and all his servants kneeled down, praising God. There, on Juan Diego's cloak, was a beautiful picture of the lady, the Virgin Mary! The bishop ordered that a church be built on Tepeyac in her honor.

When Juan arrived home that night, his uncle was well. The two men spent the rest of their lives teaching people to love God and to honor and trust the Virgin Mary.

The church at Tepeyac is still there. And inside is the miraculous picture of that beautiful woman, Mary.

123

Blessed Kateri Tekakwitha

Tekakwitha was a young Mohawk Indian girl born in what we now call New York in 1656. Her mother was a Christian Algonquin Indian, and her father was the Iroquois chief of the Turtle tribe.

The Indians believed that the meaning of their names would affect their lives. Tekakwitha means "putting all things in order." And Tekakwitha did just that. She put all things in her life in order because she put God first.

When Tekakwitha was only four years old, her mother, father, and baby brother died of a terrible disease called smallpox. Tekakwitha survived, but the disease left marks on her body and damaged her eyes.

Tekakwitha's uncle became the Turtle chief when her father died. He adopted Tekakwitha into his lodge, or home. He did not believe in God — he was a pagan.

When Tekakwitha was eighteen, missionaries came from France to teach the Mohawks about the one true God. Tekakwitha was baptized and given the Christian name Kateri, which means Catherine.

Kateri's family did not like the Christians. Her relatives were very angry that she was baptized and made fun of her faith. Kateri was patient and loving to them, but she finally had to leave her home. Kateri went to live at a Christian mission in Canada.

Kateri worked hard there and prayed often. One day she made a special promise to Jesus. She said she would not marry anyone; instead, she would spend her life praying for everyone and doing acts of kindness. She put her life in order, with God first and his people next. She put herself last.

Kateri died of an illness in 1680, when she was only twenty-four years old. Her last words were "Jesus! Mary! I love you." We can pray to her for help in putting our lives in order, with God first.

SAINT FRANCES CABRINI

Frances Cabrini grew up in Italy, a country in Europe, about 150 years ago. She was baptized the day she was born because she was such a tiny, sick baby. She was never very healthy, but she became one of the greatest missionaries ever.

When Frances was thirteen, a missionary came to town and talked about spreading God's Word in China. Frances dreamed of becoming a missionary there. She studied hard in school and grew up to become a teacher. She started a group of sisters who, like Frances, wanted to be missionaries.

Frances went to Rome to talk to the pope about her ideas. She wanted to go with the group of sisters to China, but the pope told her she should do good work in America instead. The United States was new then. Many people had moved there from Italy, and they needed help building hospitals and schools and caring for children without families.

But Frances had a secret: She was frightened of the ocean. To get to America, she would have to ride for weeks on a ship across the ocean. She didn't know what to do.

Finally, Frances prayed to God. Then, even though she was very scared, she got on the ship with the other sisters, and they crossed safely to America. Over the years, Frances crossed the ocean twenty-five times — even though she was still afraid!

Frances and her sisters helped many people in America. She stayed and became a citizen, an official member of America. Frances Cabrini is the first U.S. citizen to become a saint.

You can ask Saint Frances Cabrini to pray with you to God for courage even when you are frightened.

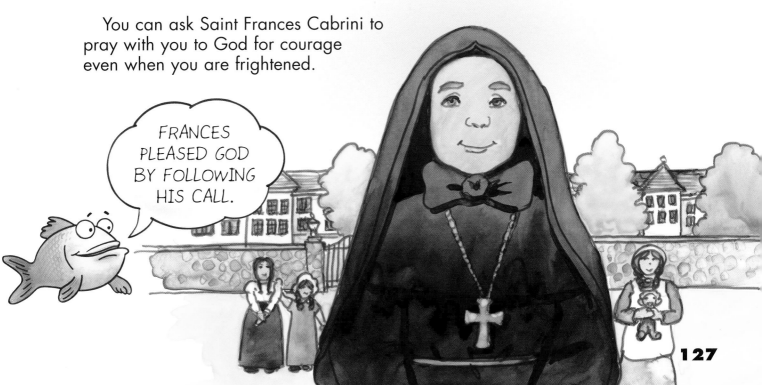

FRANCES PLEASED GOD BY FOLLOWING HIS CALL.

VI.

THIS WE BELIEVE

THE POPE AND HIS HOME, THE VATICAN

The pope is the leader of the Catholic Church for the entire world. The first pope was Saint Peter, Jesus' friend and apostle. He became the first leader of the Church when Jesus said, "on this rock I will build my church."

Saint Peter chose other Christians to help him lead the Church, and together they decided Linus would follow Saint Peter as the next pope. Each pope after Saint Peter has been chosen by Church leaders in the same way. This is called "apostolic succession."

Our current pope is John Paul II. He took this name when he became pope, to show respect for other popes who had these names. But when John Paul II was a young boy, his name was Karol Wojtyla. He lived in the country of Poland. Karol loved to read and write, and he loved God very much. When he grew up, Karol became a priest, caring for God's people in his community. Later Karol was made a bishop. As a bishop, he took care of a much larger group of God's people and was the leader of the priests in the area. Other Church leaders saw his good work and holiness and chose him to be pope, the highest office in the Catholic Church. Now he serves all the people of God.

The pope travels the world to spread God's Word. But his home is the Vatican in Rome, Italy. The Vatican is a huge group of buildings, much too big for just one man to live there! Many people who work for the Church also live at the Vatican.

Visitors often bring wonderful gifts to the pope, so the Vatican created a museum to share these treasures with everyone. There is also a giant library at the Vatican, filled with many very old and important books of the Church. Some people spend most of their lives studying these old books to help us learn more about the Christians who lived before us.

The pope is often very busy, surrounded by his helpers, members of the Church, and visitors. But the pope can also spend time alone in quiet prayer in the Vatican's beautiful gardens.

THE CHURCH: GOD'S HOME AND OURS

The word "church" can mean two things. First, it means the people of God, Catholics who believe in Jesus Christ and follow him. This meaning of the word "Church" is often written with a capital "C."

The word "church" also refers to the building in which we worship God. This meaning of the word "church" starts with a lowercase "c."

A church building is God's home on earth. It is our home, too. God is there in the Blessed Sacrament of the Eucharist. Many beautiful churches have been built all over the world. Some are very large and grand. Some are small and humble. For Catholics, God is there in a special place called the "tabernacle" of every church.

Reconciliation Room

Stations of the Cross

Baptismal Font

Holy Water Font

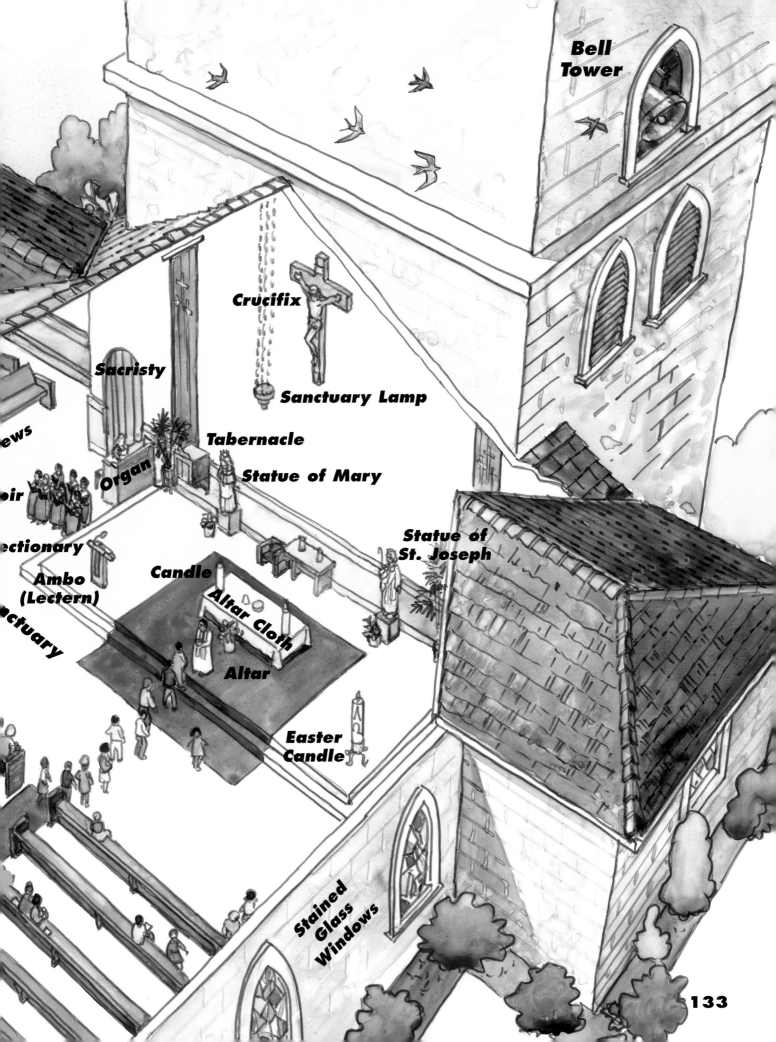

Bell Tower

Crucifix

Sacristy

Sanctuary Lamp

Tabernacle

Organ

Statue of Mary

ews

Statue of
St. Joseph

oir

ectionary

Candle

Ambo
(Lectern)

Altar Cloth

ctuary

Altar

Easter
Candle

Stained
Glass
Windows

THE MASS

Every weekend and on some special days, we go to church to honor God. There we celebrate Holy Mass. It is the ancient prayer of our faith. At Mass we remember how Jesus died and rose again. We receive Jesus, and we give ourselves to God.

When we celebrate Mass, many Catholics follow a set of instructions called the "Roman rite." The Roman rite tells us what prayers should be used at Mass and what should happen during Mass. This set of instructions is based on the way the first Roman Christians held Mass.

Other Catholics celebrate Mass using other rites. These rites are based on the way that Christians in the East and other parts of the world celebrated the death and resurrection of Jesus long ago.

These rites celebrate the same thing. We are like one big family. We are all Catholic.

Patrick and the Shamrock: The Trinity

Patrick was a young boy who lived in the Roman part of Britain about 360 years after Jesus' birth. When Patrick was sixteen, he was kidnapped and taken to Ireland. There he was forced to be a slave, caring for his master's flock of sheep. After six years, Patrick escaped and went back to Britain. He studied hard to became a priest and, later, a bishop.

In his heart, though, Patrick seemed to hear the Irish people calling him back. He asked to be allowed to go to Ireland as a missionary. He wanted to bring the Good News of the one true God to the Irish people.

Patrick worked among the Irish people for twenty-nine years. He wanted them to understand God's love for them. One day, one of the Irish kings challenged him. "You talk about one God, but then you say God the Father, God the Son, and God the Holy Spirit. It seems as if there are three Gods! Which is the one true God?"

Patrick looked around and saw a lovely green shamrock growing at the king's feet. He picked the clover and showed it to the king. "Look," said Patrick, "the one true God is like this shamrock. It is only one leaf, but it has three parts. God is only one God in three persons: the Father, the Son, and the Holy Spirit."

Then, thanks to Patrick's lesson with the humble little shamrock, the king was able to understand the Holy Trinity: one God in three persons.

Patrick taught the Irish many other lessons. He became the best-loved bishop of the Irish people. Later, people all over the world came to love this great saint and his easy way of teaching about the faith.

Patrick is the patron saint of Ireland. His feast day is March 17. On that day, in many places, people wear green shamrocks or clothing in honor of this great saint.

THE CREED

A creed is a prayer that lists the important things all the members of a religion believe in. Catholics say a creed at Mass called the Nicene Creed. This creed was written by the Roman emperor Constantine and the bishops at their meeting in the year 325 called the Council at Nicaea. Another ancient creed Catholics sometimes say is called the Apostles' Creed. Members of several other faiths, such as the Anglican Church and many Protestant churches, also say the Apostles' Creed.

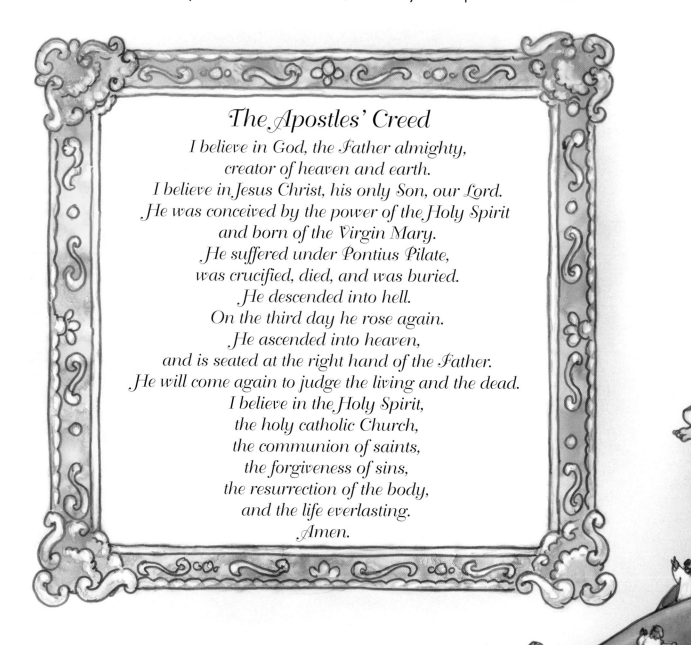

The Apostles' Creed

I believe in God, the Father almighty,
creator of heaven and earth.
I believe in Jesus Christ, his only Son, our Lord.
He was conceived by the power of the Holy Spirit
and born of the Virgin Mary.
He suffered under Pontius Pilate,
was crucified, died, and was buried.
He descended into hell.
On the third day he rose again.
He ascended into heaven,
and is seated at the right hand of the Father.
He will come again to judge the living and the dead.
I believe in the Holy Spirit,
the holy catholic Church,
the communion of saints,
the forgiveness of sins,
the resurrection of the body,
and the life everlasting.
Amen.

Jesus' Great Promise
(John 6:47)

Jesus made a great promise to his people. He said, "Truly, truly, I say to you, he who believes has eternal life."

If we live as good Christians here on earth and believe in God's Word, our souls will go to heaven to live with God forever. Jesus gave us this great gift – everlasting life – by dying on the cross for our sins. His death made up for those sins that were keeping us from entering heaven.

If we live a good life on this earth, we can live again forever in happiness with God. Hallelujah!

THE COMMUNION OF SAINTS: ONE BIG FAMILY

As God's children, we are like one big family. This family includes Christ's followers here on earth, as well as those who have died. It is known as the communion of saints.

Those of us in the communion of saints who are living in this world are called the Pilgrim Church, because we are like pilgrims traveling toward our final home, in heaven with God.

Some in the communion of saints have to make a stop in their journey to heaven. These people died with some kind of sin staining their soul, so they have to spend time in purgatory. In purgatory, souls are purified and made clean before they see Jesus. We pray for the souls in purgatory so they can go to heaven, and they can pray for us, too. We call these souls the Holy Souls, or the Church Suffering.

Some souls are already in heaven. They are pilgrims who have reached the end of their journey. We call all these souls in heaven the Church Triumphant. These members of the communion of saints are joyful to have reached our true home.

THE SAINTS, OUR FRIENDS

Throughout history, there have been special people who loved God all their lives and tried to do everything the way God wanted them to.

Other people started out sinfully, but completely changed their lives and asked God to forgive them.

Still others, called "martyrs," faced a lot of trouble for being Christians but decided that they would rather be killed than turn away from God.

When they died, the souls of these people went straight to heaven to live with God forever. We call these people "saints." The saints are our friends in heaven. We can talk to them in prayer, try to live like they did, and ask them to ask God to help us.

Saint Joseph's Big Job

Joseph was a strong, kind carpenter in Nazareth. His job was to build furniture and other things out of wood for the people of Nazareth. Joseph was engaged to be married to a lovely young girl named Mary.

One night, an angel came to Joseph and told him a great secret. The angel said Mary was going to have a baby. She would be the mother of the new king, the savior of Israel, their people. This new king would redeem the people and wash away their sins.

Joseph was worried. He thought maybe Mary already had a husband.

But the angel knew at once what Joseph was thinking. "Joseph, son of David, do not fear to take Mary as your wife, for that which is conceived in her is of the Holy Spirit," the angel said. "She will bear a son, and you shall call his name Jesus, for he will save his people from their sins."

So Joseph and Mary were married. When they had to travel to Bethlehem, Joseph made Mary comfortable on the long journey and found a warm stable where Baby Jesus could be born.

While they were there, an angel came to warn Joseph of danger, so the new father took Mary and the baby to Egypt, where they would be safe until they could return to their home in Nazareth.

Joseph cared for Baby Jesus, played with the little boy, and taught Jesus how to be a carpenter and make things out of wood. Joseph also taught Jesus the Jewish law, and took him to the temple.

All his life, Joseph was a good husband to Mary and father to Jesus. We call him the foster father of our Lord. Now Saint Joseph is with his family again in heaven.

Just as Joseph took care of the holy family on earth, he helps take care of God's great family, the Church. Ask Saint Joseph to help you grow up in God's love, just as he helped Jesus!

Saint John Bosco and the Boys

Saint John Bosco was a happy little boy in Italy. He loved to have fun and learned to do all kinds of tricks, juggling three balls at once and walking a tightrope high in the air. John also had a kind heart and wanted to help other people know how much God loved them. When he grew up, John became a priest.

In Italy, a priest is called Don. Soon all the people were taking about the kind Don Bosco.

One day, Don Bosco found a young boy hiding in the church, crying. The boy was wearing ragged clothes, and he was very hungry. The boy was an orphan. He had no mother or father to take care of him.

Don Bosco's heart nearly broke when he saw this boy. "Children should be happy and cared for," he thought. "Well, young fellow, come and help me say Mass and then we shall have some lunch," Don Bosco said.

Sadly, the boy shook his head. "I cannot do that. I do not know how," he said.

Don Bosco's heart hurt even more. Not only was the boy a poor, hungry orphan, but he also didn't realize that God loved him.

Don Bosco taught the boy how to help at Mass. He gave him clean clothes and a big dinner. Then the priest gave the boy a place to stay.

When the boy went to sleep, Don Bosco took a walk around town. He realized that there were many young boys who had no one to take care of them. Other poor boys never went to school because it was very expensive. Some boys who were very poor stole food and ended up in jail. People said these boys were bad. But Don Bosco didn't think so. He knew that if someone would feed them and teach them how to work, they would not have to steal their food. Most of all, Don Bosco knew that God loved these boys very much. Someone needed to tell them that.

Don Bosco asked his mother to help care for these boys. He asked some friends to help him teach the children in a free school. He would teach the boys about God. He would teach them how to be happy again.

Even today, the followers of Don Bosco help poor children all over the world. The Salesian priests and brothers teach them the love of God as well as skills so they can find work when they grow up.

Saint Mary Mazzarello

Don Bosco saw that many young girls were also poor orphans. They needed help, too. He visited a woman named Mary Mazzarello.

"Mary," he said. "I need someone to help take care of poor girls, just as my friends and I are taking care of the boys. Will you give your life to God by helping his poor daughters?"

Mary looked at the great saint in surprise. "Don Bosco," she said, "I will gladly do all I can to help God by helping these girls. But how can I teach them anything? I, too, am a poor girl. I never went to school. I cannot even read!"

The great saint just laughed. He knew that God had chosen Mary for this work. "Well then," he said, "you will just have to learn to read at once!"

And that is what Mary did. She studied hard and learned to read so she could teach the poor girls of Italy. Like Don Bosco, Mary asked friends to help her in her work. Today, the Daughters of Mary Help of Christians care for poor girls all over the world.

SAINT DOMINIC SAVIO

One of Don Bosco's students, Dominic Savio, decided he wanted to be a saint. While the other boys were playing ball, Dominic said his Rosary. When the other boys were off having fun, Dominic went into the church and prayed. At supper, while the others were eating their fill, Dominic ate only bread and water. This went on for several days, until Don Bosco saw what was going on. He called Dominic to him.

"What are you doing?" the saint asked the young boy.

"I want to be a saint," Dominic answered.

Don Bosco laughed and laughed. "Oh, Dominic," he said. "Certainly you should pray and say your Rosary. Sometimes you should do penance for your sins by just eating bread and water. But that is not the way to become a saint! You are a young boy, and God does not ask you to do these things all the time."

"Well, then," Dominic said, "how can I become a saint?"

Again the great saint laughed. "Dominic, God loves to see boys and girls happy. Enjoy yourself. There are two things that will help you to be a saint. Love God with all your heart and keep away from sin!"

Dominic listened to his wise teacher. He began to play as well as to pray. He loved God with all his heart and tried his best never to sin. And one day, he got his wish: Today he is Saint Dominic Savio. He is a special saint for young people, reminding them that we can all become saints.

SAINT THÉRÈSE'S LITTLE WAY

Thérèse Martin lived in a large and happy family in the countryside of France in the late 1800s. She dreamed of being a great missionary when she grew up, traveling the world to spread the Good News of God's love.

But when Thérèse was an adult, she gave her life to God. She joined a group of nuns called the Carmelites, promising to spend all her life in Carmel praying for others. As a cloistered nun, Thérèse would not be traveling to far-off places.

Of course the nuns, also called "sisters," did other things besides praying. They made things to sell, so they could earn money to buy their food. Each of the sisters had chores to do. They cleaned their home, washed their dishes and clothes, and grew a garden. There was time for the sisters to relax, too. They sang or read, painted, sewed, and visited with the other sisters. But their main job was to adore God and to pray to him for people all over the world.

Thérèse had promised not to leave her convent, so she gave up her dream of being a missionary. She still thought about ways to help the missions, though. As a nun, Thérèse did not have any money to send, but she asked her friends outside the convent to help. She also prayed for the missionaries, asking God to protect them. She wrote them letters, telling them how wonderful it was that they were sharing God's Word.

Even though she never left her convent, Thérèse became a great missionary. Today she is the patroness, or special protector in heaven, for all the missions of the world.

Thérèse also loved nature. One day she was admiring the big, beautiful roses and lilies that people picked and brought to decorate the altar, when she noticed some little daisies. They were much smaller, but they still were a beautiful part of God's creation. Thérèse realized that not all flowers could be lovely roses or lilies, but that there was a place for the humble little daisies, too. She is known as the "Little Flower" because of this.

"I am not rich," she thought, "so I cannot bring big presents to God. But I can bring him little things. I can try to do even the smallest things for him because I love him. My small things will make him happy because I am doing them just for him!"

Thérèse called this her "Little Way to Heaven." She knew that if we do even the smallest things with love for God, he will be happy. Because of her simple, but important ideas about doing everything for love of God, we call St. Thérèse a "Doctor of the Church."

GOD LOVES TO HEAR FROM US.

PRAYER: A CONVERSATION WITH GOD

We spend lots of time talking to the people we love. We can show our love for God by talking to him in prayer. We can tell God how great he is. We can thank him for the wonderful things in our lives. We can ask God to forgive our sins, and we can ask him to help us and others.

When we pray we also listen, to hear what God is telling us about our lives.

Jesus taught us a very special prayer, called the Our Father.

Our Father

Our Father, who art in heaven,
hallowed be thy name.
Thy kingdom come,
thy will be done,
on earth as it is in heaven.
Give us this day our daily bread,
and forgive us our trespasses,
as we forgive those who trespass against us.
And lead us not into temptation,
but deliver us from evil.
Amen.

At Mass, we add another part to this prayer. We say:

For the kingdom, and the power, and the glory are yours, now and forever.

We also pray before we eat a meal, asking God to bless it and us.

A Prayer Before Meals

Bless us, O Lord,
and these thy gifts,
which we are about to receive,
from thy bounty,
through Christ our Lord.
Amen.

We can pray to the angels and saints to help us. You may already know one prayer to Mary, called the Hail Mary. It is on page 42 of this book.

We also can ask our own guardian angel to protect us. This is a great prayer to use at bedtime or whenever you are feeling frightened.

Prayer to My Guardian Angel

Angel of God,
my guardian dear,
to whom God's love
entrusts me here,
ever this day,
be at my side,
to light and guard,
to rule and guide.
Amen.

There are many other prayers we can use to talk to God. But we don't always have to say a prayer that someone else wrote. God loves it when we talk to him with our own words. Simply tell him what is on your mind and in your heart.

The Sacraments: Signs of God's Love

Jesus gave us seven signs, or special gifts of grace, to help us grow in God's love. We call these the seven "sacraments."

We celebrate some of these sacraments with a special event at our church.

The Seven Sacraments
Baptism
Communion, also called the Eucharist
Penance, also called Reconciliation
Confirmation
Marriage
Holy Orders
Anointing of the Sick

At baptism, we are dipped in water or it is poured over our heads, showing that our sin is washed away and we are reborn as Catholics.

We receive the Real Presence of Jesus when we go to Communion. The bread and wine that became his Body and Blood now feed our hearts with his love.

During the sacrament of penance, we tell our sins to a priest, ask God to forgive us, celebrate his pardon, and grow closer to our Church community again.

At confirmation, the Holy Spirit comes to us and makes us strong, so we can continue the work of Jesus and his apostles. We are anointed with oil. A small amount is rubbed on our forehead, as a mark of the Holy Spirit.

Bishops, priests, and deacons receive the sacrament of holy orders, giving their lives to serve God and all his people. The community comes together to pray for them and show support for them.

In the sacrament of marriage, God joins a man and a woman to do his work and share his blessings through their family. The man and woman celebrate this bond at their wedding.

The anointing of the sick helps us heal our spirits and accept God's plan for our bodies. The priest, the sick person, and family members come together to pray, and the sick person's body is anointed with oil.

When we receive these sacraments, we are filled with God's divine grace and grow in perfection the way God wants us to.

A Year With God:
The Liturgical Calendar

You probably have a calendar in your home to keep track of your family's important days. The Catholic Church also has a calendar, called a "liturgical calendar."

The liturgical calendar reminds us of the Church's important days, called "feasts," when we celebrate Christ's birth, his death, and his rising from the dead. It also tells us when to celebrate the feasts of the Virgin Mary and of the saints, and it shows us the seasons of the Church year.

For Christians, Easter is the most important day of the year, when Jesus rose from the dead. We spend forty days praying and remembering what happened at Easter. This time to pray and prepare is called "Lent."

The next important day of the liturgical year is Christmas, Jesus' birthday. Advent is a joyful time before Christmas spent preparing for Jesus' arrival.

Sunday is the most important day of the week for the Church, because Jesus comes to us in the Eucharist at Mass. Other special feast days are spread throughout the year.

We use special colors to help celebrate the Church's feasts. The priest's clothes, called "vestments," match those celebration colors.

The priest wears white for the feast days of our Lord and our Lady, for Christmas and Easter, and for angels and some saints. The priest wears red on Palm Sunday, Good Friday, and for the feasts of the apostles and martyrs. Purple is the color for Lent and Advent. On two days during Lent and Advent, the priest wears a rose-colored vestment. He wears green the rest of the year. Black is sometimes worn at funerals, but white or purple is more popular.

There are other special clothes that the priest wears when he says Mass. The altar servers and other helpers sometimes have special clothing, too. Some of these helpers are the deacon, the Eucharistic ministers, the lector, and the cantor.

Dalmatic

Lector

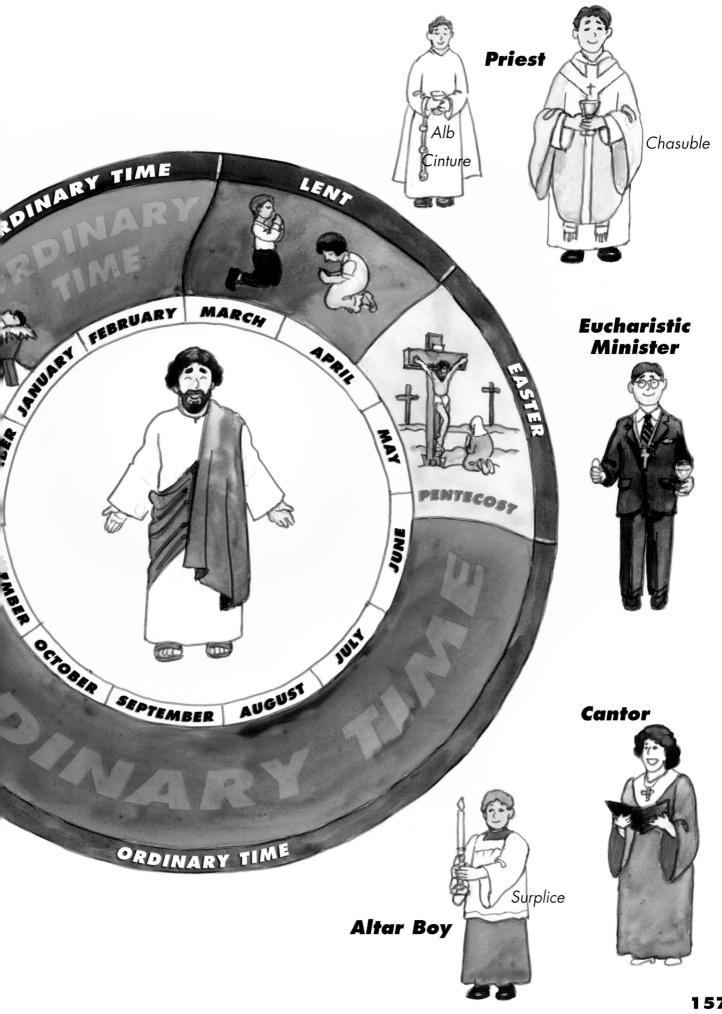

Priest

Alb

Cinture

Chasuble

Eucharistic Minister

Cantor

Altar Boy

Surplice

ORDINARY TIME

LENT

EASTER

PENTECOST

JANUARY

FEBRUARY

MARCH

APRIL

MAY

JUNE

JULY

AUGUST

SEPTEMBER

OCTOBER

ORDINARY TIME

157

WHAT WOULD JESUS DO?
THE CORPORAL AND SPIRITUAL WORKS OF MERCY

As Christians, we should always try to do helpful things that show our love for other people. Jesus told us that when we show our love for other people, it is the same as showing our love for him.

The Church tells us seven ways we can care for people's bodies and help them feel more comfortable. These are called the "corporal works of mercy."

THE CORPORAL WORKS OF MERCY
Feed the hungry.
Give a drink to the thirsty.
Give clothes to those who have none.
Shelter the homeless.
Visit the sick.
Visit the prisoners.
Bury the dead.

The Church also lists seven ways we can care for people's souls and help them feel more peaceful. These are called the "spiritual works of mercy."

THE SPIRITUAL WORKS OF MERCY
Teach those who don't know.
Correct sinners.
Give advice to those who are confused.
Show patience.
Forgive others.
Comfort the suffering.
Pray for the living and the dead.

THE JESSE TREE: A FAMILY TREE

A family often grows much like a tree. The oldest members of the family are like the roots and trunk of the tree. Their children and grandchildren are the branches spreading out as the family grows.

Many people make a Jesse tree during Advent, the time when we wait to celebrate Jesus' birth. The Jesse tree is Jesus' family tree.

To make a Jesse tree, find a large branch without leaves and place it in a container on a table. Then make symbols or pictures to represent all of the people in the Bible who lived before Jesus. Adam and Eve were our first parents, so something representing them should hang on the tree first. To represent the story of Noah, hang a rainbow or an ark on the Jesse tree. For King David, you might choose a lyre, the musical instrument he played for his sheep. Moses could be shown with the burning bush or with the Ten Commandments.

A Jesse tree is a good way to remind us of the people who lived before our promised savior, Jesus, came to earth. These people were the ancestors of Jesus.

CATHOLIC SACRAMENTALS

Sacramentals are objects and actions the Catholic Church gives us to help us remember our love for God. If we use them wisely, they can bring us gifts of grace. The sacramentals include many beautiful blessings.

A BLESSING FOR CHILDREN

May the Lord Jesus,
who loved children,
bless us and keep us in his love,
now and forever.

Amen.

Other sacramentals you may know are holy water, scapulars, holy medals, and rosaries.

CHRISTIAN SYMBOLS

Throughout time, people have used pictures or symbols to remind them of what they believe. These are some symbols Christians use:

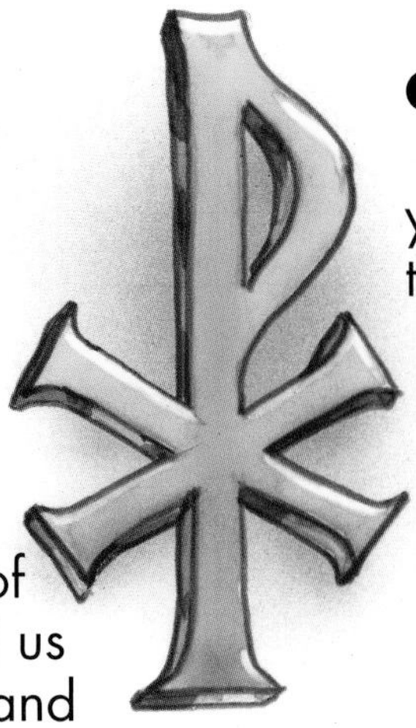

Chi Rho
This symbol is made when you put together the letters of the Greek word for Christ.

Alpha and Omega
The first and last letters of the Greek alphabet remind us that God is the beginning and the end of everything.

Lamb
Just like the lamb that was killed during the Jewish feast of Passover, Jesus was sacrificed so everyone could hope to go to heaven.

Cross
This is the main symbol of Christianity. It reminds us that God loved us enough to send his Son to die for our sins.

THIS IS WHERE I GOT MY NAME!

Ichthus
This special picture of a fish reminds us of Jesus. His apostles were "fishers of men."

Ship
The Church goes forward together, with Jesus leading at the helm, or front of the ship.

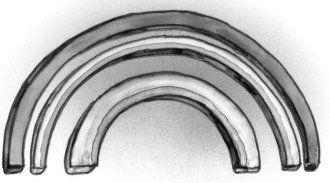

Rainbow
God sent one to Noah after the flood; it reminds us that God keeps his promises.

Butterfly
Like a butterfly coming out of a cocoon, Christ rose from the dead.

VII.

Index

About the Authors and the Illustrator

Ann Ball

A highly energetic, creative businesswoman and Catholic writer, Ann lives in Houston, Texas. She pens books and articles about modern saints and Catholic heritage and traditions. A native Texan, Ann taught school in Texas and California for many years and is delighted to now be working on more books for children. After all, "Grammaw" Ann has eight young readers for her books: Austin, Max, Michael, Victoria, Brenden, Christian, Karolyn, and Katharyn.

Julianne Will

After a decade as a writer, editor, marketing specialist, and designer at newspapers in Indiana and Colorado, Julianne has happily landed as a book editor and project manager at Our Sunday Visitor. She spends her spare time volunteering at the local art museum, studying to be a personal trainer, and seeing things anew through the eyes of her six-year-old daughter, Mia. A cradle Catholic, Julianne is now eagerly sharing her faith as a volunteer in her parish's religious education program.

Kevin Davidson, Illustrator

A graduate of the prestigious Art Center College of Design in Pasadena, California, Kevin divides his time between family and his dual careers as an award-winning watercolorist and as an illustrator. Over the years, he has worked on a variety of projects, from children's books to murals to large housing-development project illustrations for the advertising industry. In his spare time, Kevin enjoys the outdoors, watercolor painting, singing in his church's choir, painting sets for Christmas productions, Bible reading, nature walks with his wife, June, and restoring their 1901 Victorian home in Old Towne Orange, California.